LIVE YOUR LIFE
ON PURPOSE

Other Books by Pat Sendejas:

Letting Go to Create a Magical Life
A Guide to Your Personal Freedom

Coming in 2012

Do It Yourself Feng Shui Guide
Your Resource for Health, Wealth,
& Happiness

LIVE YOUR LIFE ON PURPOSE

DISCOVER YOUR FENG SHUI PERSONALITY:
THE PEOPLE & SPACES THAT SUPPORT YOU

PAT SENDEJAS

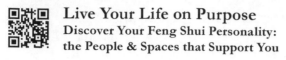

Live Your Life on Purpose
Discover Your Feng Shui Personality:
the People & Spaces that Support You

Balboa Press books may be ordered through booksellers or by contacting:

Balboa Press
A Division of Hay House
1663 Liberty Drive
Bloomington, IN 47403
www.balboapress.com
1-(877) 407-4847

Because of the dynamic nature of the Internet, any web addresses or links contained in this book may have changed since publication and may no longer be valid. The views expressed in this work are solely those of the author and do not necessarily reflect the views of the publisher, and the publisher hereby disclaims any responsibility for them.

The author of this book does not dispense medical advice or prescribe the use of any technique as a form of treatment for physical, emotional, or medical problems without the advice of a physician, either directly or indirectly. The intent of the author is only to offer information of a general nature to help you in your quest for emotional and spiritual well-being. In the event you use any of the information in this book for yourself, which is your constitutional right, the author and the publisher assume no responsibility for your actions.

Edited by: Victoria Giraud

Graphic Designs by: Gary Mann

Cover Photo from the Hubble Telescope and NASA

ISBN: 978-1-4525-4662-9 (e)
ISBN: 978-1-4525-4663-6 (sc)
ISBN: 978-1-4525-4661-2 (hc)

Library of Congress Control Number: 2012901580

Printed in the United States of America

Balboa Press rev. date: 3/23/2012

Acknowledgement

To my husband Sal for his love and constant encouragement as he inspired me to continue to move forward to complete this book. Special thanks to my mother who has always believed in me, telling me I could do anything I set my mind on. I greatly appreciate her enthusiasm to spread the word about my work, always looking for new ways to promote me. To my editor and good friend, Victoria Giraud: I could not imagine creating a book without her. Her humor and joy of life is contagious and made this project fun. To Gary Mann, a talented graphic designer, one of his many talents, who brought my book to life with his determination to provide the best graphics for my readers. I am grateful and was surprised to find Gary on the other end of my e-mails working along with me in the wee hours of the morning to complete this book in a timely manner. To James Bond, my business coach—Gary and I refer to him as 007—I appreciate his encouragement and help to bring clarity to my message that we are all unique and have a special gift to give the world. To my longtime friend Tawnia Sodergren who gave me my first book on Feng Shui, introducing me to what has become my passion. To so many of my students and clients who kept asking when this book would be available: I appreciate your support and encouragement. My deepest thanks to you all and to the Universe for bringing you into my life for the best gift of all, your love!

~

Table of Contents

Preface

This book is intended to help you understand who you are: your innate personality qualities and your passions and strengths, which help you live your life on purpose. You will gain awareness about why certain relationships work for you and others seem more challenging, and how the right environment and certain relationships can best support you. Once you have this information, you can make the choices that align with your innate personality and experience your true power.

Based on the Traditional Feng Shui, this fascinating knowledge dates back to ancient times. Users of Feng Shui are able to make an instant shift in their perspective, allowing them to be more understanding of others, and more positive about their own choices. This nature science is based on the natural elements in the world and how each of us relates to those elements.

Most people are surprised to learn that the first step in applying the principles of Feng Shui is to understand the individual and their preferences, just like an interior designer must first interview the client to find out how a space will be used, since form follows function. This book is step one on the road to living your purpose and knowing who you are before you select or design your home, work, or play spaces.

Although many of these ideas may be new to you, keep an open mind. When information feels right to you, it is usually time for you to hear it and/or apply it. In order to truly be yourself, it is important to honor what feels and works best as you get in touch with how people and experiences feel to you.

My book, which focuses on people, their relationships to each other and to their spaces, is meant to be fun, informative, and easy to understand. I give you simple tips for making changes in your environments and your life choices that impact you positively and help you align with your life purpose now.

Introduction

During almost a decade of studying Architecture, Environmental and Interior Design, and operating my own interior design business since 1977, I had never heard about Feng Shui. In 1996, a friend gave me a book about the fascinating subject of Feng Shui, an ancient science based on the compass and mathematic calculations. I was so intrigued by the book I immediately wanted to learn more and to teach it.

Not long ago, this very old practice was unknown in the US, but it is now taught in design programs at numerous colleges and universities across the country. My wish to teach this subject came true when I was invited to teach Feng Shui at a local community college.

In China, it was a very secretive practice passed from one generation to the next among the country's rich and powerful leaders. Feng Shui is also known as an intuitive art: people claim they can feel the positive energy known as ch'i, and problematic energy called sha.

Charting people for their compatibility and innate gifts is my favorite part of Feng Shui. As I studied it, I learned a lot about myself and about the people in my life, their likes, dislikes and career choices. To my surprise, placing beds according to the individual's best sleep direction, and setting up offices and desks with a person's best facing direction for concentration and meditation all seemed to have a positive impact on my family and my clients.

I now use Feng Shui when I create architectural plans for new construction and remodels, particularly important for room placement, and matching the energy of the space with the function or activity intended by the client. If a client wants a home office, it is important to choose the area of the home with energy that is good for the expansion of business and wealth. An elderly person needs to occupy a room that supports good health.

The lengthy complex rules of this practice may strike our modern culture as odd, but its practice has proven effective for positive change. For example: if a home's front door faces oncoming traffic at the end of a street (as in a dead end), it is rarely fortunate for the home's occupants. Round pillars are better than square ones, which have sharp edges. Ceilings are best when flat, well lit, and without beams.

Feng Shui was very foreign to me at first; I thought it was just a system that could be changed to fit any situation in order to validate life events. I encouraged myself to keep an open mind, and events in my life proved to me how useful this valued system can be.

The traditional compass school of Feng Shui uses mathematical calculations based on the year a building's construction is completed. I learned that nature has reoccurring cycles of change that repeat every nine years, and the study of these cycles over thousands of years has resulted in a pattern of predictability, which is used to determine reoccurring energy and/or events. The different cycles of energy are: the productive cycle, the dominant cycle, and the reductive cycle. These cycles are the basis of deciding what remedy will bring balance to an environment and even a relationship in order to create harmony and flow. As a typical Western example: those who watch the stock market or the real estate market understand there are cycles of profits and cycles of loss.

Over the years I have discovered many American entrepreneurs use Feng Shui in confidence to avoid the misunderstandings associated with the practice, and that several well-known members of the US Congress have had Feng Shui done for their offices.

In a 2008, Daily News article, Gilda L. Ochoa, associate professor of sociology and Latino studies at Pomona College, said using Feng Shui at MacDonald's in Hacienda Heights was "a perfect example" of global capitalism's co-opting people's culture. She added, "It is a microcosm of a changing United States." Newspaper reports surfaced about Disney redoing all of their amusement parks according to Feng Shui principles after building their theme park in Hong Kong.

In August 2000, the Los Angeles Business Journal reported, "Two years ago negative energy stalked the City of Gardena. Bad business deals had created a budget deficit of $4.7 million, and a former city manager was suspected of embezzlement. Things got so bad that then-Assistant City Manager Mitch Lansdell decided to call in a Feng Shui practitioner. Lansdell claimed he was now a believer in the benefits of Feng Shui, as he reported that by June 30, 2000, the changes made to the environment based on Feng Shui were the reason the city's deficit was reduced to $2.9 million."

As I continued to study Feng Shui, I learned how its influences and cycles of energy were affecting my family. In Feng Shui, all people fall into a natural element category based on their year of birth, which designates their innate connection to one of the following elements: fire, earth, metal, water, or wood. These element categories also determine whether a person and/or a house are designated as East Group or West Group. When a person's category matches the house category, their life experience is enhanced with more success in a career, relationships, and health.

The home my husband and I and our two sons moved into in 1993 was a spacious newly built custom home in the beautiful Santa Monica Mountains of California. It was a West Group home, which supported my husband, our oldest son, and myself. It did not support my youngest son, an East Group type. It made sense; our younger son had more challenges in this home, whereas our West Group older son had an easier life here. When I remembered our previous home, I realized my younger son had had a more positive experience. I did the calculations and discovered that home had been an East Group, a match for him for the first twelve years of his life, whereas my older son, who was part of the West Group category, faced more difficulties in that earlier home.

Even though our home in the mountains seemed to support three out of four family members based on the East/West Group Theory, I soon discovered that the home's permanent energy, captured when it was built in 1992, was not supportive for health or finances for any of us. In addition, the 1998 Feng Shui yearly energy reading indicated there was separation coming into the heart of all houses; in combination with the home's permanent energy, our home had the potential for some form of pain and death energy. We decided to sell our home and were pleased to find a buyer who was a West Group type and would be supported by the house. Coincidentally, she was in the process of a divorce and the separation and "death of the old" visiting energy was coming that next year and would support her actions.

The new yearly energy arrives around February 5th each year. Before we moved, however, we couldn't avoid experiencing the death and pain energy. As the yearly energy continues it becomes a little stronger each month. On March 23, 1998, my nephew called to ask me if I knew a Los Angeles City Fire Department helicopter had crashed earlier that morning. My husband, Sal, a firefighter who worked at the Van Nuys Airport fire station, often flew on these copters. Television news wasn't giving out details and I couldn't get anyone to answer the fire station phone. Two hours passed, and in that time I told myself that I had applied all I was learning about Feng Shui, and I had done everything possible to create peace and harmony in our house to help prevent any harm to my family. I had to let go and wait for news.

Shortly after, my husband called and verified the helicopter from his station did go down while transporting a twelve-year-old girl after a car accident. The crash killed the girl, one of the firefighters, and the two paramedics who were treating her. Our family felt great sadness over the deaths. It helped us to see how important it is to love and appreciate each other in the moments we are together; we never know how long that may be. My husband attended seven memorial services over the next ten days and then we moved from the house. Meant to be? Most likely, as fate is another consideration in Feng Shui, and with all my remedies in place, we will never know what might have occurred without those remedies in place.

Chapter One

Discover Your Feng Shui Authentic Self & Live More Confidently, Joyfully, & in Your Passion

Want to create harmony within your relationships? Discover your unique personality and how you relate to others. Understand better why people think or act the way they do. **The Productive Cycle** illustrated in *Figure 1*, represents how the Five Elements in nature support each other. People also support each other in a similar manner.

Why do certain relationships go smoothly while others are a struggle? Once you find your Element, one of the five, you'll discover a major key to understand and change your life for the better.

Your element is associated with your innate personality type, based on your year of birth. The chart shows us how these elements work in nature. As Fire burns, it leaves behind ashes and replenishes the Earth. Earth supports Metal as Metal comes out of the Earth. Metal strengthens Water as seen when condensation forms on the Metal of an automobile. Water helps plants and trees grow, which supports Wood. Wood helps Fire burn more intensely when Wood is added to a campfire. These cycles constantly reoccur and are symbolic in relationships.

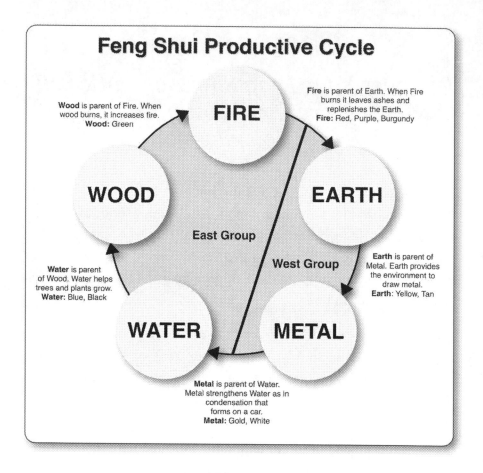

Figure 1

Why do certain relationships go smoothly while others are a struggle? Once you find your Element, one of the five, you'll discover a major key to understand and change your life for the better.

Your element is associated with your innate personality type, based on your year of birth. The chart shows us how these elements work in nature. As Fire burns, it leaves behind ashes and replenishes the Earth. Earth supports Metal as Metal comes out of the Earth. Metal strengthens Water as seen when condensation forms on the Metal of an automobile.   Water helps plants and trees grow, which supports Wood. Wood helps Fire burn more intensely when Wood is added to a campfire.   These cycles constantly reoccur and are symbolic in relationships.

When I charted Tara Lipinski, the 1998 Gold Metal Ice Skating champion, born June 10, 1982, I found her to be a Metal-Yang. It was perfectly fitting that Tara had been skating with Metal ice skates on frozen Water (the parent of Water) for years.   It was also no wonder Tara won the Gold in Nagano, Japan, a landscape of mountains; Metal is supported by Earth.

To discover your element, search the **Birth Chart** in *Figures 2 through 5* for your birth year. The element for males is listed in the center column and the female elements are on the right. Each year starts on February 5.

Note: Those born before February 5 would use the previous year to determine their correct element.   Example: Anyone born January 16, 1937 would select the year Feb. 5, 1936 to Feb. 4, 1937.   Males would be Water Yin and females Earth Yang.   Once you discover your own personal element, you will be able to look up your unique personality description in this chapter, illustrated by the personal element charts *Figures 6 through 13*.   Be sure to note your Yin or Yang type along with your element.

At the same time you may want to make a list and locate others such as: family members, your siblings, children, partner, parents, business associates and close friends. This chapter provides those people who are most compatible to you.

CHINESE BIRTH CHART 1912 - 1945

BIRTH DATE RANGE	MALE TYPE / ELEMENT/ NO			FEMALE TYPE / ELEMENT/ NO		
Feb 5, 1912 - Feb 4, 1913	Yin	Metal	7	Yang	Earth	8
Feb 5, 1913 - Feb 4, 1914	Yang	Metal	6	Yang	Fire	9
Feb 5, 1914 - Feb 4, 1915	Yin	Earth	2	Yin	Water	1
Feb 5, 1915 - Feb 4, 1916	Yin	Wood	4	Yin	Earth	2
Feb 5, 1916 - Feb 4, 1917	Yang	Wood	3	Yang	Wood	3
Feb 5, 1917 - Feb 4, 1918	Yin	Earth	2	Yin	Wood	4
Feb 5, 1918 - Feb 4, 1919	Yin	Water	1	Yang	Earth	8
Feb 5, 1919 - Feb 4, 1920	Yang	Fire	9	Yang	Metal	6
Feb 5, 1920 - Feb 4, 1921	Yang	Earth	8	Yin	Metal	7
Feb 5, 1921 - Feb 4, 1922	Yin	Metal	7	Yang	Earth	8
Feb 5, 1922 - Feb 4, 1923	Yang	Metal	6	Yang	Fire	9
Feb 5, 1923 - Feb 4, 1924	Yin	Earth	2	Yin	Water	1
Feb 5, 1924 - Feb 4, 1925	Yin	Wood	4	Yin	Earth	2
Feb 5, 1925 - Feb 4, 1926	Yang	Wood	3	Yang	Wood	3
Feb 5, 1926 - Feb 4, 1927	Yin	Earth	2	Yin	Wood	4
Feb 5, 1927 - Feb 4, 1928	Yin	Water	1	Yang	Earth	8
Feb 5, 1928 - Feb 4, 1929	Yang	Fire	9	Yang	Metal	6
Feb 5, 1929 - Feb 4, 1930	Yang	Earth	8	Yin	Metal	7
Feb 5, 1930 - Feb 4, 1931	Yin	Metal	7	Yang	Earth	8
Feb 5, 1931 - Feb 4, 1932	Yang	Metal	6	Yang	Fire	9
Feb 5, 1932 - Feb 4, 1933	Yin	Earth	2	Yin	Water	1
Feb 5, 1933 - Feb 4, 1934	Yin	Wood	4	Yin	Earth	2
Feb 5, 1934 - Feb 4, 1935	Yang	Wood	3	Yang	Wood	3
Feb 5, 1935 - Feb 4, 1936	Yin	Earth	2	Yin	Wood	4
Feb 5, 1936 - Feb 4, 1937	Yin	Water	1	Yang	Earth	8
Feb 5, 1937 - Feb 4, 1938	Yang	Fire	9	Yang	Metal	6
Feb 5, 1938 - Feb 4, 1939	Yang	Earth	8	Yin	Metal	7
Feb 5, 1939 - Feb 4, 1940	Yin	Metal	7	Yang	Earth	8
Feb 5, 1940 - Feb 4, 1941	Yang	Metal	6	Yang	Fire	9
Feb 5, 1941 - Feb 4, 1942	Yin	Earth	2	Yin	Water	1
Feb 5, 1942 - Feb 4, 1943	Yin	Wood	4	Yin	Earth	2
Feb 5, 1943 - Feb 4, 1944	Yang	Wood	3	Yang	Wood	3
Feb 5, 1944 - Feb 4, 1945	Yin	Earth	2	Yin	Wood	4

Figure 2

CHINESE BIRTH CHART 1945 - 1978

BIRTH DATE RANGE	MALE TYPE / ELEMENT/ NO			FEMALE TYPE / ELEMENT/ NO		
Feb 5, 1945 - Feb 4, 1946	Yin	Water	1	Yang	Earth	8
Feb 5, 1946 - Feb 4, 1947	Yang	Fire	9	Yang	Metal	6
Feb 5, 1947 - Feb 4, 1948	Yang	Earth	8	Yin	Metal	7
Feb 5, 1948 - Feb 4, 1949	Yin	Metal	7	Yang	Earth	8
Feb 5, 1949 - Feb 4, 1950	Yang	Metal	6	Yang	Fire	9
Feb 5, 1950 - Feb 4, 1951	Yin	Earth	2	Yin	Water	1
Feb 5, 1951 - Feb 4, 1952	Yin	Wood	4	Yin	Earth	2
Feb 5, 1952 - Feb 4, 1953	Yang	Wood	3	Yang	Wood	3
Feb 5, 1953 - Feb 4, 1954	Yin	Earth	2	Yin	Wood	4
Feb 5, 1954 - Feb 4, 1955	Yin	Water	1	Yang	Earth	8
Feb 5, 1955 - Feb 4, 1956	Yang	Fire	9	Yang	Metal	6
Feb 5, 1956 - Feb 4, 1957	Yang	Earth	8	Yin	Metal	7
Feb 5, 1957 - Feb 4, 1958	Yin	Metal	7	Yang	Earth	8
Feb 5, 1958 - Feb 4, 1959	Yang	Metal	6	Yang	Fire	9
Feb 5, 1959 - Feb 4, 1960	Yin	Earth	2	Yin	Water	1
Feb 5, 1960 - Feb 4, 1961	Yin	Wood	4	Yin	Earth	2
Feb 5, 1961 - Feb 4, 1962	Yang	Wood	3	Yang	Wood	3
Feb 5, 1962 - Feb 4, 1963	Yin	Earth	2	Yin	Wood	4
Feb 5, 1963 - Feb 4, 1964	Yin	Water	1	Yang	Earth	8
Feb 5, 1964 - Feb 4, 1965	Yang	Fire	9	Yang	Metal	6
Feb 5, 1965 - Feb 4, 1966	Yang	Earth	8	Yin	Metal	7
Feb 5, 1966 - Feb 4, 1967	Yin	Metal	7	Yang	Earth	8
Feb 5, 1967 - Feb 4, 1968	Yang	Metal	6	Yang	Fire	9
Feb 5, 1968 - Feb 4, 1969	Yin	Earth	2	Yin	Water	1
Feb 5, 1969 - Feb 4, 1970	Yin	Wood	4	Yin	Earth	2
Feb 5, 1970 - Feb 4, 1971	Yang	Wood	3	Yang	Wood	3
Feb 5, 1971 - Feb 4, 1972	Yin	Earth	2	Yin	Wood	4
Feb 5, 1972 - Feb 4, 1973	Yin	Water	1	Yang	Earth	8
Feb 5, 1973 - Feb 4, 1974	Yang	Fire	9	Yang	Metal	6
Feb 5, 1974 - Feb 4, 1975	Yang	Earth	8	Yin	Metal	7
Feb 5, 1975 - Feb 4, 1976	Yin	Metal	7	Yang	Earth	8
Feb 5, 1976 - Feb 4, 1977	Yang	Metal	6	Yang	Fire	9
Feb 5, 1977 - Feb 4, 1978	Yin	Earth	2	Yin	Water	1

Figure 3

CHINESE BIRTH CHART 1978 - 2011

BIRTH DATE RANGE	MALE TYPE / ELEMENT/ NO			FEMALE TYPE / ELEMENT/ NO		
Feb 5, 1978 - Feb 4, 1979	Yin	Wood	4	Yin	Earth	2
Feb 5, 1979 - Feb 4, 1980	Yang	Wood	3	Yang	Wood	3
Feb 5, 1980 - Feb 4, 1981	Yin	Earth	2	Yin	Wood	4
Feb 5, 1981 - Feb 4, 1982	Yin	Water	1	Yang	Earth	8
Feb 5, 1982 - Feb 4, 1983	Yang	Fire	9	Yang	Metal	6
Feb 5, 1983 - Feb 4, 1984	Yang	Earth	8	Yin	Metal	7
Feb 5, 1984 - Feb 4, 1985	Yin	Metal	7	Yang	Earth	8
Feb 5, 1985 - Feb 4, 1986	Yang	Metal	6	Yang	Fire	9
Feb 5, 1986 - Feb 4, 1987	Yin	Earth	2	Yin	Water	1
Feb 5, 1987 - Feb 4, 1988	Yin	Wood	4	Yin	Earth	2
Feb 5, 1988 - Feb 4, 1989	Yang	Wood	3	Yang	Wood	3
Feb 5, 1989 - Feb 4, 1990	Yin	Earth	2	Yin	Wood	4
Feb 5, 1990 - Feb 4, 1991	Yin	Water	1	Yang	Earth	8
Feb 5, 1991 - Feb 4, 1992	Yang	Fire	9	Yang	Metal	6
Feb 5, 1992 - Feb 4, 1993	Yang	Earth	8	Yin	Metal	7
Feb 5, 1993 - Feb 4, 1994	Yin	Metal	7	Yang	Earth	8
Feb 5, 1994 - Feb 4, 1995	Yang	Metal	6	Yang	Fire	9
Feb 5, 1995 - Feb 4, 1996	Yin	Earth	2	Yin	Water	1
Feb 5, 1996 - Feb 4, 1997	Yin	Wood	4	Yin	Earth	2
Feb 5, 1997 - Feb 4, 1998	Yang	Wood	3	Yang	Wood	3
Feb 5, 1998 - Feb 4, 1999	Yin	Earth	2	Yin	Wood	4
Feb 5, 1999 - Feb 4, 2000	Yin	Water	1	Yang	Earth	8
Feb 5, 2000 - Feb 4, 2001	Yang	Fire	9	Yang	Metal	6
Feb 5, 2001 - Feb 4, 2002	Yang	Earth	8	Yin	Metal	7
Feb 5, 2002 - Feb 4, 2003	Yin	Metal	7	Yang	Earth	8
Feb 5, 2003 - Feb 4, 2004	Yang	Metal	6	Yang	Fire	9
Feb 5, 2004 - Feb 4, 2005	Yin	Earth	2	Yin	Water	1
Feb 5, 2005 - Feb 4, 2006	Yin	Wood	4	Yin	Earth	2
Feb 5, 2006 - Feb 4, 2007	Yang	Wood	3	Yang	Wood	3
Feb 5, 2007 - Feb 4, 2008	Yin	Earth	2	Yin	Wood	4
Feb 5, 2008 - Feb 4, 2009	Yin	Water	1	Yang	Earth	8
Feb 5, 2009 - Feb 4, 2010	Yang	Fire	9	Yang	Metal	6
Feb 5, 2010 - Feb 4, 2011	Yang	Earth	8	Yin	Metal	7

Figure 4

CHINESE BIRTH CHART 2011 - 2044

BIRTH DATE RANGE	MALE TYPE / ELEMENT/ NO			FEMALE TYPE / ELEMENT/ NO		
Feb 5, 2011 - Feb 4, 2012	Yin	Metal	7	Yang	Earth	8
Feb 5, 2012 - Feb 4, 2013	Yang	Metal	6	Yang	Fire	9
Feb 5, 2013 - Feb 4, 2014	Yin	Earth	2	Yin	Water	1
Feb 5, 2014 - Feb 4, 2015	Yin	Wood	4	Yin	Earth	2
Feb 5, 2015 - Feb 4, 2016	Yang	Wood	3	Yang	Wood	3
Feb 5, 2016 - Feb 4, 2017	Yin	Earth	2	Yin	Wood	4
Feb 5, 2017 - Feb 4, 2018	Yin	Water	1	Yang	Earth	8
Feb 5, 2018 - Feb 4, 2019	Yang	Fire	9	Yang	Metal	6
Feb 5, 2019 - Feb 4, 2020	Yang	Earth	8	Yin	Metal	7
Feb 5, 2020 - Feb 4, 2021	Yin	Metal	7	Yang	Earth	8
Feb 5, 2021 - Feb 4, 2022	Yang	Metal	6	Yang	Fire	9
Feb 5, 2022 - Feb 4, 2023	Yin	Earth	2	Yin	Water	1
Feb 5, 2023 - Feb 4, 2024	Yin	Wood	4	Yin	Earth	2
Feb 5, 2024 - Feb 4, 2025	Yang	Wood	3	Yang	Wood	3
Feb 5, 2025 - Feb 4, 2026	Yin	Earth	2	Yin	Wood	4
Feb 5, 2026 - Feb 4, 2027	Yin	Water	1	Yang	Earth	8
Feb 5, 2027 - Feb 4, 2028	Yang	Fire	9	Yang	Metal	6
Feb 5, 2028 - Feb 4, 2029	Yang	Earth	8	Yin	Metal	7
Feb 5, 2029 - Feb 4, 2030	Yin	Metal	7	Yang	Earth	8
Feb 5, 2030 - Feb 4, 2031	Yang	Metal	6	Yang	Fire	9
Feb 5, 2031 - Feb 4, 2032	Yin	Earth	2	Yin	Water	1
Feb 5, 2032 - Feb 4, 2033	Yin	Wood	4	Yin	Earth	2
Feb 5, 2033 - Feb 4, 2034	Yang	Wood	3	Yang	Wood	3
Feb 5, 2034 - Feb 4, 2035	Yin	Earth	2	Yin	Wood	4
Feb 5, 2035 - Feb 4, 2036	Yin	Water	1	Yang	Earth	8
Feb 5, 2036 - Feb 4, 2037	Yang	Fire	9	Yang	Metal	6
Feb 5, 2037 - Feb 4, 2038	Yang	Earth	8	Yin	Metal	7
Feb 5, 2038 - Feb 4, 2039	Yin	Metal	7	Yang	Earth	8
Feb 5, 2039 - Feb 4, 2040	Yang	Metal	6	Yang	Fire	9
Feb 5, 2040 - Feb 4, 2041	Yin	Earth	2	Yin	Water	1
Feb 5, 2041 - Feb 4, 2042	Yin	Wood	4	Yin	Earth	2
Feb 5, 2042 - Feb 4, 2043	Yang	Wood	3	Yang	Wood	3
Feb 5, 2043 - Feb 4, 2044	Yin	Earth	2	Yin	Wood	4

Figure 5

Now that you know your element type, refer to the **Productive Cycle Chart** in *Figure 1* to find the location of your personal element. Notice the element that supports your personal element. Example: Wood is supported by Water. You will have a very compatible relationship when your element is the same or located adjacent to another person's element type. When there is one element missing between two elements on the **Productive Cycle Chart** the relationship may be more challenging and less compatible. According to the **Dominant Cycle Chart, Chapter 5,** *Figure 20*, one person will be more dominant. To bring balance to the relationship, refer to the **Productive Cycle** and bring into the relationship the one missing element. Such as: when an Earth and Water type are in a relationship, according to the **Productive Cycle**, the missing element is Metal.

To bring about a more harmonious relationship, this couple might choose to work out at the gym together where there is the element of metal, go bike riding, travel in metal planes, or automobiles, and/or trains. All of these examples are ways to bring metal into the relationship. Sometimes a child with a Metal personal trigram comes into the family to bring about balance between two people. Sometimes the house type will be of the element to bring about compatibility. It will be important to bring in the missing element to have harmony in that relationship. **Chapters 6-8** help to explain how to bring balance to different relationships. Find your element in *Figures 6 through 13* to see the details and innate qualities associated with your personal element type.

Note: There are two types of Earth, Metal, and Wood; one is Yin and the other is Yang. There is one Fire, Yang, and one Water, Yin. These two elements Fire and Water are illustrated on the **Yin and Yang Symbol** in **Chapter 5**. Make sure you note on the **Birth**

Chart if your element is Yin or Yang. Select the chart below that reflects your specific element with Yin or Yang type.

Personality Types:

The Metal Yang types have historically been selected as leaders of China. They are organized, make good decisions, and are good leaders. They are also very competitive and like to win. Usually, they own their own companies and if not, they are managers or create a department where they can be in charge. When I spoke to an Interior Design Organization about innate personality types, one woman told me afterward she discovered she was a Metal Yang and finally understood why she had been elected to the position of president only three months after she joined the organization! See *Figure 6.*

METAL YANG: West Group (W, NE, SW, <u>NW</u>)*

Element:	Hard Metal
Yin/Yang:	Yang
Tendencies:	Head of company, head of household, leader
Symbol:	Heaven
Body Parts:	Head and lungs
Supported By:	Earth (colors of Earth; yellow, tan, beige)
Supports:	Water
Colors:	Gold, white
Number:	6
Orientation:	Northwest

Figure 6

The Yin Metals love bringing joy and humor to any gathering and are often referred to as "party animals." I consulted with a couple who were grandparents. As we gathered around the dining table in their home, they gave me the birth dates, and I began to chart all twelve of their grandchildren to discover the unique personalities of each. One of their granddaughters charted as a Metal Yin. The Metal Yin is known to be a good speaker, a sales person, and is a good communicator. I told them their granddaughter could even become a TV anchor person, or reporter. Her grandparents laughed and then told me her parents had nicknamed her Gabby. See ***Figure 7***.

METAL YIN: West Group (NW, SW, NE, <u>W</u>)*

Element:	Soft Metal
Yin/Yang:	Yin
Tendencies:	Fun loving, good communicators, good in sales, referred to as the "party animal"
Symbol:	Marsh
Body Parts:	Mouth, chest, teeth
Supported By:	Earth (colors of Earth; yellow, tan, beige)
Supports:	Water
Colors:	Gold, white
Number:	7
Orientation:	West

Figure 7

A young father who is a **Water Yin** shared with me that his idea of relaxation is riding a jet ski to Catalina, twenty-six miles off the coast of California. When he reaches the island of Catalina, he puts a metal air tank on his back and goes scuba diving. I was not surprised to learn his personal element is water. He is just doing what feels natural to him, and since metal supports water, it is no wonder this young man enjoys scuba diving supported by a metal tank on his back. See **Figure 8**.

WATER YIN: East Group (SE, E, S, <u>N</u>)*

Element:	Water
Yin/Yang:	Yin
Tendencies:	Diplomatic, great negotiator
Symbol:	Water
Body Parts:	Ears, blood, kidneys
Supported By:	Metal (colors of Metal; gold, white)
Supports:	Woods - Yin and Yang
Colors:	Blue, black
Number:	1
Orientation:	North

Figure 8

The Wood Yang is known as being kind, generous, and secretive, plus is a great business confidant. When my older son was getting ready to leave his job for another position, he mentioned to me he told a co-worker he would be leaving soon. I asked him if it wouldn't have been better to tell his boss first. He proceeded to remind me that his friend is a Wood Yang and is kind, generous and secretive, being a good business confidant. There was not much I could say in response to his reasons. See *Figure 9*.

WOOD YANG: East Group (S, N, SE, E̲)*

Element:	Hard Wood
Yin/Yang:	Yang
Tendencies:	Secretive, kind, generous, tends to be explosive
Symbol:	Thunder
Body Parts:	Throat and feet
Supported By:	Water (colors of Water; blue, black)
Supports:	Fire
Colors:	Green
Number:	3
Orientation:	East

Figure 9

The **Wood Yin** is the traveler, also referred to as "the Wind." I had a client who was an experienced speech therapist who traveled from school to school, perfect for her element type. She told me how much she loved her job traveling from school to school. The following year she phoned to say she had taken a promotion at the district administration office because it offered more money and she was looking forward to her advancement. Six months later I ran into her, and she told me she had gone back to her previous job traveling from school to school because she missed the freedom and movement. See *Figure 10*.

WOOD YIN: East Group (N, S, E, SE)*

Element:	Soft Wood
Yin/Yang:	Yin
Tendencies:	Restless, called "The Traveler", quiet, sensitive, and intuitive.
Symbol:	The Wind
Body Parts:	Thighs and buttocks which relate to tree trunks
Supported By:	Water (colors of Water; blue, black)
Supports:	Fire
Colors:	Green
Number:	4
Orientation:	Southeast

Figure 10

The Fire Yang types are known to be good teachers. You see their hearts through their eyes, and they often have red hair, a fire color. I met a woman who had just turned fifty at one of my seminars. When we charted each person in attendance, she admitted her element was Fire and she told the class that she recently left her corporate job to do what she had always longed to do, become an elementary school teacher! See *Figure 11*.

FIRE YANG: East Group (E, SE, N, <u>S</u>)*	
Element:	Fire
Yin/Yang:	Yang
Tendencies:	Determination, drive, a workaholic
Symbol:	Fire
Body Parts:	Eyes and heart (You see their heart through their eyes
Supported By:	Wood/Plants (colors of Wood; Green)
Supports:	Earths - Yin and Yang
Colors:	Red, purple, burgundy, maroon
Number:	9
Orientation:	South

Figure 11

The Earth Yin is supportive and nurturing; because they tend to be very concerned about others, they are often referred to as a "mother hen." Also known as "mother earth," they have a natural ability to make friends with all different types of people from different cultures. I consulted on a home for a couple, who wanted me to help get their son's room ready for his return from a prestigious university. They were concerned because their Earth Yin son was spending more time helping other students than working on his own studies. They decided to move him to a local university for his final years of study. I told them it would be important to help him find a career where he could support and nurture others because this was who he innately was. My client shared with me a year later that her son had chosen international studies, which was perfect for the Earth Yin type who relates to all cultures. Other satisfying careers for this Earth Yin could be counseling, physical therapy, nursing, or working as a flight attendant. See ***Figure 12***

EARTH YIN: West Group (NE, W, NW, SW)*	
Element:	Soft Earth
Yin/Yang:	Yin
Tendencies:	Very caring, nurturing, "mother hen" tends to worry about others before self.
Symbol:	Earth (relating to "mother earth")
Body Parts:	Abdomen or stomach
Supported By:	Fire (colors of fire; red, purple, burgundy, maroon)
Supports:	Metals - Yin and Yang
Colors:	Yellow, tan, beige
Number:	2
Orientation:	Southwest

Figure 12

The Earth Yang has to be creative. They are happiest when they are creating, whether it is painting a bathroom or writing a book. They are the most creative of all the elements making them good interior designers and architects. They also need variety and the opportunity to meet lots of different people. When I was working to get clear about what career I wanted to pursue, someone told me to take my own test. I realized they were referring to the Productive Cycle-5 Elements Theory. As a true Earth Yang, I looked back over my life and saw how I pursued every creative endeavor I could. At age seven, while spending the night with a friend, I suggested we rearrange her parents' living room furniture. I took every creative class I could: flower arranging, cake decorating, making my own clothes, and stained glass window design, to name a few, and I spent nine years in formal education for design and architecture. It always amazes me how this science reveals so much about our innate nature. See *Figure 13*.

EARTH YANG: West Group (SW, NW, W, NE)*

Element:	Hard Earth
Yin/Yang:	Yang
Tendencies:	Very creative, enjoys variety & people, tends to be stubborn
Symbol:	Mountain
Body Parts:	Bony parts: Knees, elbows, vertebrae
Supported By:	Fire (colors of fire; Red, purple, burgundy, maroon)
Supports:	Metals - Yin and Yang
Colors:	Yellow, tan, beige
Number:	8
Orientation:	Northeast

Figure 13

Once the element type for each person is determined, the buildings placement on the land reveals its compatibility to the individuals working and living within.   Determining your building type is covered in **Chapter 7**.

Chapter Two

Feng Shui Secrets in the 21ˢᵗ Century Used by Big Business to Generate More Clients, Wealth & Productivity

Feng Shui is not a religion. It is the traditional Chinese practice of utilizing the energy around us to create balance and flow in all areas of our life. When balance is achieved, life flows effortlessly and a feeling of well-being occurs.

There are many different types of Feng Shui practices. I see them popping up daily in order to sell anything from bedroom accessories and makeup to pet supplies. Although I primarily use the **Traditional Compass School** of Feng Shui, I utilize many other theories of Feng Shui when I consult with clients. I incorporate the **Form School Theory**, **Yin and Yang Principles** based on the well-known book of *I-Ching*, the **Five Element Theory**, the **Eight Personal Trigrams**, and the **East/West Group Theory**. Each of these theories is covered in detail in later chapters.

The **Form School** incorporates careful observations about the land and its relationship to the position of the building (home or office, etc.) on the land. The environment around a building impacts the user client the most and is the first consideration in a Feng Shui consultation after charting the occupants for their element type. The most ideal situation is to select the land before a building is built, which gives the opportunity to choose the best directions based on the future occupants, and ensures the building/home supports them. With an existing structure remedies are selected from the five elements to improve the environment, inside and out, with consideration for the building's energy and location.

The Compass School method utilizes a compass to determine the eight directions in and around a building. A compass reading is used to determine the compatibility of the building with the client, and the best supportive directions for a client's bed or desk chair, for instance. The **Compass School** incorporates the **Yin and Yang Theory**, which emphasizes the importance of balance and relies on the five elements of nature: fire, earth, metal, water, and wood, combined with the theories of mutual creation and mutual destruction.

Incorporated into the **Compass School** is a system of using eight different personal Trigrams that determine the best directions and types of buildings for individuals. Once an individual has determined their element category, referred to as a Trigram, it reveals the four best supportive bed directions, the four best supportive directions a chair should face, and the four best types of buildings unique to the individual that best enhance health, attract romance and love, and promote prosperity for that person! Understanding the cycles of nature as being productive, reductive, and/or dominating helped me to understand the relationships I have created with friends and family, as well as the relationship I have with a building or an environment where I choose to live or work.

A building may be supportive to one person, and not as supportive to another, depending on the **East or West Group** of the individual, and the **East or West Group** of the building. It's ideal when the building is a match with the individual's personal trigram/element. **Chapter 7** explains how to determine if your building supports you according to the **East/West Group Theory**.

Feng Shui is an analytical system developed by a centuries-old cumulative tradition based on meticulous observations over thousands of years of the elements of nature and its relationships in the natural environment, as well as information about an individual.

The most important elements of Feng Shui are:

1)   Your destiny is based on your personality and the innate qualities you are born with. You cannot change destiny.

2)   Luck – it is believed that some are born with luck.

3)   The flow of your life and how you respond to what happens to you is revealed through Feng Shui.

4)   Karma – referred to as cause and effect.

5)   Hard work – martial arts, which is having discipline to achieve more, is an example.

The Traditional Feng Shui is based on the Chinese mathematical system developed by ancient scholars. Because math is a universal language, I feel I can depend upon this practice. This Chinese practice was used to cool homes, utilizing water along with air currents.   It was intended to protect the emperor from the elements of nature and from his enemies and to maintain good health for him and his family.   Observing nature shows us how to live in balance and in harmony with one another and with our environment. In China, according to Feng Shui principles, marriages were matched for their compatibility and leaders chosen according to the eight personality Trigram types.

Architect Frank Lloyd Wright is best known for utilizing all the elements of nature in his buildings. He often incorporated the earth element, as in the stone he used in the Hollyhock House or the brick in other buildings. He positioned the fireplace in the center of his homes, and imaginatively used water in the famous home called "Falling Waters." Wood was employed in the custom design of his furnishings and metal in his lighting accessories and decorative items. Utilizing the energy around and within us is creative. Frank Lloyd Wright was a perfect example of Feng Shui and creativity in action! He studied Chinese architecture and this is apparent in his own architecture and furnishings.

Feng Shui is a specialized method of harmonizing the manmade environments in which we live and the calculation of time and space. The environment affects us tremendously: the trees, which give us oxygen, the earth that surrounds us with its life-giving magnetic field, the cars and the buildings, and even the pollution. The buildings we live/work in have a great effect on us, from the modern scientific sense when we hear about dangerous asbestos to the emotional responses we have to light, colors, sound, and textures.

Because of my architectural background, I like the fact Feng Shui had been historically established for years and is based on mathematics. I did not want to rely on a practice based on superstition or something that was a fad. I picked a teacher who was born in China and selected from his siblings to study Feng Shui when he was six years old. He followed a relative, who had been a renowned Feng Shui Master for years, to learn Feng Shui by observation. This practice was handed down from family to family, through word of mouth, and it was a very secretive practice. The Traditional Feng Shui, which I practice, is a science incorporating ancient philosophies, astronomy, geography, the environment, physics, mathematics and magnetic fields that are all around us and in every living cell.

I have often been asked if numerology is part of Feng Shui since both practices use mathematics. Much as I enjoy the study of numerology, it is not to be confused with Feng Shui. House numbers and room numbers are not greatly emphasized, but many people, intent on success, insist on incorporating the powerful Feng Shui numbers of 8 and 6 in their phone numbers and addresses. That intention can be very powerful and creative in itself.

Many traditions developed from Feng Shui. Geomagnetism pertains to the magnetic properties of the earth. Geomancy is derived from geo, meaning earth, and mancy, meaning knowledge, in the sense of predicting or foretelling. Geomancy, as defined by the New World Dictionary, is divination by random figures formed when a handful of earth is thrown on the ground, or as a line drawn at random. Geology is a study of the rocks of the earth and how they were formed, but geomancy is an esoteric way of indicating how the forces of the earth affect us. Esoteric means something is being understood by only a chosen few, is beyond the understanding of most people, and is held in great confidence.

Feng Shui is a type of Chinese geomancy, but it is not simply related to the earth. It relates to all of the factors of time, space, the environment, the building, and the individuals who occupy that building. There have been other types of geomancy from other countries. From the Chinese point of view when it is practiced in all aspects, Feng Shui involves not only space but also time. It has some relationship to Chinese astrology, but it involves how time and space interact with each other.

Traditional Feng Shui is unique. The Black Hat type of Feng Shui, for example, implies that the energy in a building is unchanging, starts with the door and always follows the same order for money or romance. I find that every building has a different placement on the land, and the visiting energy coming in each year changes, causing the energy to vary based on the directions of each building, unique to its site. The placement of entrances and bedrooms is unique to each building, and the areas where people spend the most time will have a strong impact upon that individual. Doorways and bedroom placements vary from house to house. Therefore, I have found the **Traditional Compass School** practice of Feng Shui allows for cycles of nature, the amazing variety in the universe, and in each individual.

There are many cycles that affect us. Time relates to different cycles of the universe: cycles of day and night, monthly cycles of the moon, and annual cycles that revolve around the sun. These cycles and the energies associated with them will be discussed in detail in my advanced Feng Shui book.

Chapter Three

What Powerful Chinese Emperors Knew About Feng Shui to Protect Their Family, Health, & Prosperity

Feng Shui cannot be separated from Chinese philosophy. If you have studied Chinese medicine, other Chinese philosophies, like Tai Chi, calligraphy, drawing and painting, you will see that their roots go back thousands of years. The original concept of the book of *I-Ching* was developed in prehistoric times. The *I-Ching* is a Chinese classical book that began 4,000 to 5,000 years ago, and was developed over time by different philosophers. The book is the basis of most Chinese thought and sciences. It does not belong to any one religion, but is a part of all Chinese culture.

The book title *I-Ching* translates to book of changes. Its wisdom includes such advice as: enjoy the good times, but know there won't always be good times. Find a way through the bad times as best you can, but know that nothing stays the same. I had a client who shared her view on life: "Life is like a roller coaster. When it's going up, enjoy the ride; when it's going down, hold on tight!" We can always count on change. Feng Shui came from this philosophy, but its roots go back 5,000 years. Crucial concepts were added over the years. The **Yin and Yang Theory** was developed in the pre-Christian era, about 1,000 years before Christ. **The Five-Element Theory** is estimated to have been developed 200 years before Christ.

The origin of Feng Shui as a separate Chinese science is hard to determine because it is based on secret knowledge used primarily by

Chinese emperors, who each retained a full time Feng Shui master. Feng Shui began as a way to protect the emperors of China and their families by creating and maintaining health and prosperity. Astronomers and meteorologists were also retained by the emperor to observe the environment to determine those areas most protected from nature and from enemy attacks.

In order to gain control and power, little was written down about this secret science, thus giving the emperor an advantage over those individuals challenging his wealth and security. Daughters were not taught the practice of Feng Shui so they could not share this privileged information when they married and joined their new husband's family. The information was intended to be exclusive to one family. All literature about Feng Shui was forbidden to commoners. Information was passed on through elite families from generation to generation.

The long-kept secret of Feng Shui became known to commoners when Yang, an astronomer and meteorologist to the emperor, fled the Imperial Palace with valuable information on Feng Shui during the Yellow Bandits Rebellion in 907 AD. He took his knowledge and lived in exile, hiding in the hills. He decided it was time to disseminate the knowledge to people who could "receive" it. Because he used it to help poor people make their lives easier, he became a folk hero, like a Chinese version of the English tales of Robin Hood!

When Yang left the emperor's inner circle, he began teaching Feng Shui and this knowledge began to filter out into Chinese culture. His name, Yang Yun-Song, was a nickname for "save the poor." He only took on the most intelligent students, who had to qualify first to serve a lifelong apprenticeship following the master. Eventually, the master might give his blessings, and the student could teach on their own. For many years, Feng Shui was only taught from teacher to student in a very selective, intimate way.

The practice of Feng Shui was used for family burials. If the loved one was buried correctly, according to the selection of the gravesite's sitting and facing direction, it would have a positive effect on their descendants for 180 years to follow.

Feng Shui has gained a great deal of popularity over the centuries. In China today there are millions of books on Feng Shui, and more and more books in English line bookstore shelves. Feng Shui is an extensive study that takes many years to master. There are those who call themselves a Feng Shui teacher and write a book, but it does not mean their level of study and understanding is high. To improve health and prosperity, even a beginner can comprehend and use some aspects of it. It is my intent to help the reader navigate through complex information in order to have a greater understanding of Feng Shui. In order to receive the greatest benefits, I suggest this practice be studied in depth and taken very seriously. My ***Do It Yourself Feng Shui Guide*** provides step by step instruction to determine all the energies and proper remedies for your buildings.

Chapter Four

How to Use the Yin and Yang Theory to Bring Your Life in Balance & Attract Your Most Supportive Relationships

In Feng Shui, it is very important to be aware of balance, which has the biggest impact on your environment, your relationship with family, friends, and co-workers, and especially the relationship you have with yourself. Although many people have never thought to have a relationship with themselves, it is the key to contentment and peace. The **Yin and Yang Theory** deals with the concept of balance, and offers examples of why being aware of and consciously striving to create balance in your life is so important.

Figure 14

Illustrated here in ***Figure 14***, **Yin and Yang**, has great symbolic meaning and is used to interpret energy within nature, within people, within the seasons and in many other aspects of life. The circular symbol contains a curving white shape—the Yang—on the left, and a curving black shape—the Yin—on the right, together forming a circle of balance. The Chinese read from right (Yin), to left (Yang), opposite from Western culture.

This correct symbol shows the dark Yin, with its heavy area at the bottom to the right, representing the flow of water, which seeks its lowest point downward with the help of gravity. As an example: homes located at the bottom of a hill may become flooded by water drainage from hills above, therefore proper drainage is an important concern for homes located at the lowest level of the land. In Feng Shui, homes below the street level are too Yin, and are not recommended as having positive energy. Similar to a sandbag, which is used to stop or redirect water, in this instance the home would act as a block to stop the energy at its lowest point.

Homes located below the street level are susceptible to floods and the accumulation of debris, which is negative energy, called sha, because it accumulates and becomes stagnant and has the potential to become toxic. Think of energy like flowing water to understand better how this invisible energy accumulates at your door, around your house, or in pockets of space within the environment. Consequently, space becomes quite critical to Feng Shui and to achieving balance. Positive energy that flows and moves freely is called ch'i, also spelled qi.

The white Yang energy in the symbol indicates fire. The larger portion is at the top since fire burns upward to its highest source of fuel. Wildfires, for instance, burn toward the top of a hill, and homes at the top are in the most danger.

In this symbol, Fire is Yang: hot, bright, white, active, and aggressive. Water is Yin: wet, cool, dark, flowing downward in a passive manner, always seeking the lowest point, illustrated in the next few graphics. To achieve balance in your environment, it is advantageous to select a home located between the lowest Yin area in your neighborhood, and the highest Yang area, sheltered by a mountain behind.

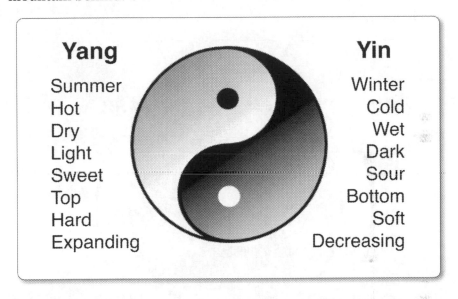

Yang

Summer
Hot
Dry
Light
Sweet
Top
Hard
Expanding

Yin

Winter
Cold
Wet
Dark
Sour
Bottom
Soft
Decreasing

Figure 15

Yin and Yang examples can be seen everywhere. The seasons are a perfect example of **Yin and Yang**. During the winter months, the seasons are more Yin with shorter daytime hours, and have more darkness and less sunshine. In contrast are the summer months of hot weather. We will often refer to summer days as scorching hot, as if to imply a fire-like, hot condition.

Refer to **Figure 16**. As you look at the symbol, you can see the summer months at the top of the symbol have more Yang energy.

Moving clockwise to the right, fall is represented by the beginning of yin, as the leaves begin to drop from the trees, and the temperature begins to decrease. The winter months are a form of Yin energy, and we experience the shortest day of the year on December 21st. Spring is the end of Yin and the beginning of Yang, when flowers begin to bloom in profusion just before the arrival of summer. Yang energy increases, and Yin energy decreases. One is not better than the other.

Figure 16

Yin and Yang are individually important and each has its purpose. Do not get confused by old TV Westerns, which implied black was bad because the villain wore the black hat, and white was good because the hero wore the white hat. In China, white and black are interpreted differently. The relationship to death is white, unlike our Western implication of white for purity and newness, seen when a newborn child wears white for their christening, for instance. For this reason brides in China do not wear white wedding gowns, they wear gowns of red to symbolize passion.

In the Eastern culture the start of Yin (dark) implies the beginning of life. *In Figure 16*, move your eye clockwise from the top of the symbol going down and around the circle. Notice how the Yin gets larger and darker, symbolic of the womb enlarging before the birth of a child. Continue around the circle, the white Yang begins only as a sliver in size. Once the child is born, the full white area signifies the development of life until its completion at the top left, before the cycle of life begins again with the Yin in the darkness of the womb before birth.

Western reading habits have caused many to change the symbol to show Yin on the left and Yang on the right, thus distorting the symbol into featuring the heavy part of the white side at the bottom and the heavy part of the black at the top, illustrated in *Figure 17*. This is definitely a misrepresentation of the symbol and a distortion of the deeper meaning of **Yin and Yang**.

Figure 17

The incorrect symbol is show in *Figure 17.*

How to Best Apply Yin and Yang

The Yin/Yang concept helps us understand and strive for balance. Whenever we are in excess of either Yin or Yang for too long a period, we start to experience stress, and our life begins to feel uncomfortable. Those who are aware can choose again to be in balance with both **Yin and Yang**. In Feng Shui, the observance of the land, the earth, and nature is our best example of how to create balance.

Yin and Yang is very important to the flow in our environments. A good way to explain Yin and Yang, as seen in the environment, is to realize that Yin is dark and with darkness we can relax and sleep. With an excess of darkness we become depressed. Yang, on the other hand, is bright and oftentimes hot. When we have the drapes wide open with lots of sunlight streaming into the environment, we may become irritable because of too much light or heat. If we become irritable or depressed and are out of balance, then we lean toward one or the other polar opposites. Becoming aware of our environment by noticing if it is too bright or too dark, or too hot or too cold, we can choose to adjust the window coverings, air conditioning or heating, bringing about a balance in our environment.

When we bring about a balance in the light or temperature of a room, we become calmer, our body experiences a more comfortable temperature, and a feeling of relaxation is created. Become aware of your surroundings; watch for environments that are too bright or too dark. When you feel at ease in an environment, become aware of what it is in your surroundings that helps you feel good. When you feel apprehensive or bothered in an environment, look for things that make you feel uncomfortable. Each person has a different reaction to their environment, which can often be explained by their personal Feng Shui Trigram and their Yin or Yang Type. Be sure to know what you prefer by developing your senses and increasing your awareness.

As you can tell from the examples of Yin and Yang energy, **Yin and Yang** are polar opposites. How can we know and appreciate light without having the contrast of darkness? Taking this theory into the human emotional experience, we can understand that choosing to forgive someone only comes after having felt hurt and pain from that person.

If life were the same, day in and day out, we would become bored, like having our favorite food every day, for every meal. Would we not become tired of that perfect food at every meal? What if you had to wear that wonderful outfit, which made you feel so special, every minute of your life? Wouldn't you become tired of the same outfit day in and day out? What do you think makes that wedding so special for the bride? That once-in-a-lifetime gown! Yang contributes to the experience of Yin. Yin contributes to the experience of Yang.

Before reading further, it may be helpful to determine if you have an innate Yin or Yang quality. Refer back to *Figures 2 through 5*, in **Chapter 1**, to determine your Yin or Yang energy type based on your year of birth, listed next to your element type. Many of you will know without looking. Yang types will tend to be giving most of the time. Yang will be drawn to a Yin Trigram in order to fulfill its desire to give or lead, bringing wholeness to the relationship. It is by being with your opposite that you can achieve a balanced relationship. And Yin types will usually form a lasting relationship with a Yang type so that they can demonstrate their true nature by calming situations, following and supporting a personal or team goal, and feeling complete with their opposite. Yin types do well being a part of a supportive team.

Note: The birth charts begin on February 5 each year because Feng Shui is based on the solar calendar, as opposed to the Chinese New Year that is on a different day each year and is based on the lunar calendar. Chinese Astrology is different from Feng Shui in that it is based on the Lunar Calendar as well.

People fall into either the Yin category or the Yang category, according to the **Eight Personal Trigrams**. The ideal relationship is between a yin type and a yang type due to the complement of opposite behaviors each brings to the relationship.

Yang people tend to be more outgoing, more exertive, and are natural at leading, planning, and making decisions. Yin type people tend to be good listeners and able to receive easily. Yin energy can bring calmness to a situation and be very supportive of Yang types. Yang types love to give and are sometimes seen as too controlling or as rescuers. They become out of balance if they become too Yang and attempt to rescue others by leading, giving too much, or planning when they have not been asked.

Yin types become out of balance when they do not ask questions or reach out to others. They may expect to always be the ones who receive. This expectation from others may help create a Yin type with a limited belief in his/her own ability to create their own abundance, becoming a victim in some cases. One cannot be a rescuer (too much Yang energy) without a victim (too much Yin energy). One cannot be a victim without a rescuer. Each is drawn together, almost as magnets to their polar opposites to create a whole, or to create an experience together. It is this experience that helps people better understand who they are and if their choices best serve them.

To stay in balance, a Yin will seek out more Yang activities, like listening to upbeat music, or participating in exertive exercise, or giving to charities. The Yang may find balance by pulling back and letting others do the giving or planning, by listening to quiet, calming music, or doing yoga or less exertive exercise such as walking. In a relationship, the person with Yang energy is usually the giver. Giving in excess without choosing to receive, takes away the opportunity to feel joy that a Yin person might feel from the experience of giving.

When we become more aware of our own innate nature, we can choose to achieve a balance within ourselves. Both types of people can come from a place of contentment and joy, being able to have both the joy of giving and the humility of receiving. Learn how to be fully aware of your actions and choose how you want to be in each moment.

In Ted Andrews book, *Animal-Speak*, he states, "If we don't receive the little things--the compliments, the assistance, etc.--the universe does not send us the big things. It is the receiving of the little things that starts the magnetic pull to bring the bigger things into your life. A predator knows how to receive. When the Earth presents a prey opportunity, it goes after it. If it doesn't, it will not eat."

How often do you say, "No, thank you" when you are offered help? Do you feel you must always be the one to give, or are you always asking others to give to you? Being aware of your own actions will help you see the part you play in bringing balance to the world.

Balance is the key to everything we do and necessary to having a harmonious life. Feng Shui emphasizes the importance of balance. Think about when life has been most challenging for you. Ask yourself, Was I working all the time? Was I so depressed that I was sleeping all the time? Was I playing so much that my work did not get done? Was I spending more money than was coming in? Was I talking so much that I missed what people were saying to me? Was I listening so much to others that I could not hear my own inner voice? In order to bring about balance in your life, become aware of areas that may be out of balance, such as: time, money, relaxation, play, work, family, sleep, and physical health (paying attention to exercise or nutrition). These are only a few areas to consider, which may help you become more aware in order to choose again, in order to bring balance into your life.

To achieve balance, be aware of how much time you spend in Yang activities and how much time you spend in Yin activities. Examples of Yang energy activities are: exercise, dancing, playing, talking, and work, activities that require action. Examples of Yin are: moments of relaxation, reading, meditating, and listening to music, listening more to others than talking yourself, massages, going to the movies and anything that requires little effort or exertion by you. You may want to list the time you spend in **Yin and Yang** activities to see how much balance you are creating in your life according to your Yin or Yang innate nature.

At other times, we will gravitate to the Yin or Yang that matches us because we have so much in common. Good friends are often of the same type and element. We can say that our friend acts like a mirror for us to see our true nature of Yin or Yang and watch how that plays out. If we find that a friend has done something to truly annoy us, usually when we look deeper, we will be able to see that same behavior within ourselves. What we see in others is usually a reflection of ourselves. The relationship is a gift to help us to better understand ourselves. When you compliment another, for instance, know that the compliment is also for you to hear and gain insight. Often, what we say to another is meant for ourselves. The relationship with another therefore helps us to identify who we are!

Remember, if you are a Yang type you will naturally do more Yang (giving) activities, and if you are Yin you will practice more Yin (receiving) activities. That is why a **Yin and Yang** relationship tends to be most compatible in the give and take that is important to any relationship. When you are aware of your energy type, you can begin to choose activities to help balance your mind, body, and spirit. When a Yang is out of balance, people around them may feel like they are being pushed or bombarded.

When a Yin is out of balance people around them may feel like they are being drained of their energy, or being asked to give more then they desire. By being told "no," the Yin or Yang will realize they have crossed the line and gone out of balance. If they do not get what they want, they may choose to stop the behavior and go back into balance, or go on to find someone else who allows them to push or take, therefore never learning from the relationship how to have more balance, and improve their relationships and who they are.

In summary, people and buildings fall into two major categories: Yin or Yang. If your personal type is a Yin, for example, you may enjoy dimmer lights and a quiet environment. If your personal type is Yang, you may require more light (yang energy) and may enjoy brighter colors and more noise in your environment. Sometimes I have noticed the opposite will occur. My husband, being of the Yin energy, likes upbeat, more Yang-type music, whereas I, being a Yang energy, will often prefer softer slower, more Yin-type music. We are gravitating to our opposites probably to bring about balance at that time. The slower-paced music will tend to slow down my Yang qualities, and the faster paced music will tend to perk up his Yin qualities.

Sometimes, we become so accustomed to our environment, we no longer realize it has become out of balance. How could we not see what is happening to us each day in our immediate environment? Stress or just old habits creates a lack of attention to the moment. By not observing our thoughts we separate our minds from our bodies. Our body comes and goes, but our mind is somewhere else. By putting our thoughts on anything other than the moment and our immediate environment, we escape. We escape by thinking about the past, which is more yin, or by thinking about the future, more yang. By being out of balance with our thoughts, we miss the present moment and experiences.

Have you ever spent time with someone who is always talking about the past? The past is a safe place to think about because we know what occurred. It will never change because it has already occurred. Have you ever been with someone who always talks about the future? The future is a dream, and it can be changed at any moment. We can control the dream of the future because it has not occurred. It can be anything we want it to be.

It takes discipline to stay in the present moment. It is the art of training your mind to always be in balance with your body and what it is doing. For many of us that's difficult because we have conflict about how we feel and what we have been taught. We have formed automatic responses without thinking. Many people tell me they feel guilty when they take time to relax. I know I did as well. Why does that happen if you are choosing for yourself in each moment what you desire? It's because we are living in the past, listening to what the voices told us under different conditions. Living in the past is safe, like a child who turns to a parent for guidance and directions. As adults, we sometimes forget we have the opportunity to decide for ourselves. Drawing from our own experience and feelings in the moment allows us to make decisions that support who we have become. We can choose to have balance and create peace. When people complain they don't have enough time, it's because their choices and thoughts have created that reality.

I had been a person who did not feel I had enough time to do all the things I wanted to do. First, I changed my thought about it. I began to state, "I am pleased at the abundance of time I have." To my surprise, I then found an abundance of time and found myself almost bored with so much time! I realized how my thoughts put into motion the energy that produced my reality. The mind can be used to make logical decisions based on the emotions of the body. Bringing the mind and the emotions together in each moment causes the spirit to soar! It can raise your level of energy. Although doing what others tell us can be safe, it sends a message to our emotions that they are wrong, and a message to our mind that it is not able to make a decision.

We have been given a mind to logically decide what is best for us, to access information, and to provide us with ideas for problem solving. If we rely on the voices of the past, the mind cannot do what it has been designed to do. The body is a meter determining our emotions; we must be present to be aware of the body. When we ignore or deny our natural emotions: fear, sadness, joy, anger, jealousy, resentment, love, and guilt, we deny our true inner spirit and never get those feelings resolved in order to enjoy the balance and peace of mind we long for.

Our bodies demonstrate forms of **Yin and Yang** in many ways. If we go all day without food, we become very Yin; the stomach decreases in size, the hot juices are no longer needed and the body stops producing them. If we begin to eat, we can achieve a balance in the body, unless we continue to eat to a point of excess, throwing us out of balance again. How simple life becomes when we strive for balance. It is like breathing, balancing the inhaling and exhaling, all of which is done automatically. Every time we choose an excess of anything, we begin to go out of balance.

Being out of balance can be one way to escape. The big question to ask ourselves is, "What are we trying to escape from?" Only when we decide what it is that we want to escape from can we choose something different. Awareness of your emotions, and the way the mind is thinking about those emotions, will lead to clarity. Being honest about our feelings is the best way to begin. Never allow guilt to rule, because guilt is a wasted emotion. There are no accidents.

All events happen to give us information about our desires and ourselves so that we can make choices that work for us.

When we fully understand how important opposites are to each other, we begin to appreciate the silence after a long day of noise. We appreciate the laughter of children when we have been in long periods of solitude. Perspective is King. Your perspective about something is yours alone. No one else can come from your experience to have your perspective. You and only you can know what feels best for you. Your perspective is the only thing that matters as you choose your experiences throughout each day. Having a relationship with yourself in order to create balance is essential in finding your own peace. To be your own best friend is the best thing you can do for yourself, your family, and our society. The wise person understands and knows that feelings cannot be debated or argued. As **Yin and Yang** exist together in the same space, others do not have to be wrong for you to be right!

Notice in the **Yin and Yang Symbol**, *Figure 14*, the small black circle within the white, and a small white circle within the black. In every Yin there is always some Yang, and in every Yang there is always some Yin. Even if you are not in a serious and committed relationship with another, you are still in a relationship with yourself. Being in a relationship with yourself will help you become aware of both the **Yin and Yang** within you. If you have determined yourself to be a Yang type, then you will be more active and outgoing. Without a partner you will crave that opposite Yin energy and bring it to you by increasing your nurturing nature, giving yourself more downtime activities, or gravitating toward someone in your life with that Yin energy. The Yin type will do the same, craving more Yang activities or friendships in order to bring about a balance within.

Until you understand and accept yourself for who you are, you may not find a successful relationship. Accepting and allowing opposites to exist is the key to achieving a balance in your relationship. When I see a couple together, one a Yin, the other a Yang, I know they are being true to themselves, drawing in their opposite in order to complement themselves to achieve a balance. In our personal relationships, having a combination of **Yin and Yang** energy is truly a gift. It's an even bigger gift when it falls within the same element, which I will discuss in the next chapter.

Chapter Five

Apply the Five Elements & the Cycles of Nature to Relax, Recharge, & Improve Your Relationships

There are five individual elements in nature: Earth, Metal, Water, Wood, and Fire. When observed in nature these five elements teach us a great deal about balance and provide insight into how that balance is achieved. Feng Shui is based on creating balance to achieve a state of harmony and that information, when applied to our own relationships and environments can bring about a new awareness, helping us to see others, as well as ourselves, in a different perspective. Often this new awareness has helped to heal relationships, providing understanding and compassion for others. Buildings have eight types that fall into these five element categories. By identifying your element and the element of the building, compatibility is determined.

People also fall into one of the eight elements, called Trigrams, based on their year of birth. I have listed each element in the order of their **Productive Cycle** compatibility, illustrated in *Figure 18*. The illustration shows how the elements in nature support each other. In order to keep this book simple and easy to understand, I have not listed the Chinese names for each Trigram. If you would like to learn more about these Trigrams and their actual Chinese name, refer to the in-depth book of *I-Ching*, which is the foundation for the science of Feng Shui Personality types.

Beginning with the earth element and moving around the chart clockwise, you will see the following elements:

Earth: Energy Type: Yin

Earth: Energy Type: Yang

Metal: Energy Type: Yin

Metal: Energy Type: Yang

Water: Energy Type: Yin

Wood: Energy Type: Yang

Wood: Energy Type: Yin

Fire: Energy Type: Yang

As listed above and progressing around the chart, there are two Earths: a Yin and Yang. There are two Metals: a Yin and a Yang. There is one Water element, a Yin. There are two Woods: a Yin and a Yang. There is one Fire element: a Yang. Notice how the chart goes from Yin to Yang consistently. The swing from **Yin and Yang** is always occurring, reinforcing that things are always changing. Refer to *Figures 2 through 5 - Birth Charts* in **Chapter 1** to find the element in nature related to your year of birth.

After you have referenced your own personal element and Trigram, you can add that element of nature into your life to help you relax, give you a feeling of being connected, and an overall feeling of well-being. As I explain the **Productive Cycle**, **Reductive Cycle**, and **Domination Cycles** of nature in detail, you will become more aware of how you fit into these cycles and connect with nature as well as to other people. This information may help you seek support when you are in a low mood, recharge when you are tired, take back your power when you are being dominated, and know when to back off if you find you are the one who is dominating another.

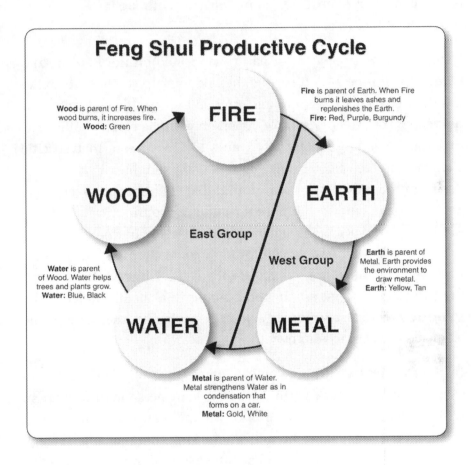

Figure 18

Notice how the **Productive Cycle** goes in a clockwise direction.

The Reductive Cycle, Illustrated in *Figure 19* goes in a counter-clockwise direction. Relationships among people are similar to these relationships with the elements. Once you have determined Trigram types among people, you can determine if the relationship is productive, reductive, or dominant (also thought of as being transformational).

Note: where your element of nature is located on the **Productive Chart**, in *Figure 18*. It reveals the relationship you have to all the different elements in nature and reveals the specific elements that best support you. For example, a person with the element of Fire as their personal Trigram usually wants to incorporate that specific element into their homes, but may not understand why. They often desire a fireplace in their home, and if that is not possible, they may go camping to enjoy a campfire, or add a fire pit to their backyard. A fire element person is adjacent to the elements of Wood and Earth, which both have a comfortable connection to that person. Each element, as shown on the **Productive Chart**, falls between the two elements that are most harmonious to them. Refer to the **Productive Chart** to identify your element and take note of the elements adjacent to your own.

In the **Productive Chart**, notice the element of Wood to see an example of how to utilize this chart for your personal information. A Wood type person may be in or around water more than most other types. They may be active in swimming, surfing, fishing, scuba diving, or snorkeling, and also take long showers or baths one to two times a day. They would enjoy being in their own element of Wood: hiking among trees, camping in nature, or working with wood to build projects. The element of Fire, adjacent to Wood on the **Productive Chart**, might show up in the form of working with computers (computers are part of the fire element), lighting, or electrical equipment, campfires, barbecues, and cooking activities, all relating to the fire element.

The **Productive Cycle Chart**, *Figure 18*, shows how one element is the parent of another. Wood supports Fire by giving the fire element an opportunity to be more of what it is: the element providing flames for warmth and cooking purposes. As in nature, I have found that a person who represents a   parenting element in relation to another element may have a parent-child relationship with that person. It would be no accident these two came together: one wanted to be like a parent, taking on responsibilities, and the other, like a child, wanted to have fun and perhaps be taken care of.

If you study the relationships you have attracted, you may see similarities to this example. Sometimes we see this parent-child relationship with a first-born person married to a person who ranked in the family as the youngest or only child.   In the parent-child type relationship, the parent type is learning from the child-type to relax, have more fun and play, and the child-type is learning from the parent-type to be more responsible and self-reliant.

A parent-child relationship may result in one person being the domineering, controlling one with the other consistently being the irresponsible jokester. In this situation neither understands the other's perspective and approach to life. Combining these types of approaches equally can bring balance to a relationship with neither person feeling cheated of their point of view and style of living. Neither way is incorrect unless obligations are ignored or stress builds up and results in illness. Ideally, it would be best to play both the parent and the child role equally to have more balance in our lives. Remember to nurture the magical child within you.

The **Reductive Cycle** illustrated in *Figure 19*, contains the elements of the **Productive Cycle** executed in the reverse direction. By going counter-clockwise, we find each element is reduced. For example, water is being reduced as wood and plants use water for their nourishment. You can better understand the relationships in your life by using the **Reductive and Productive Cycles**. First chart the elements of your family, friends and business associates to see how many people in your life may tend to reduce or increase your energy depending on the placement of your element and theirs.

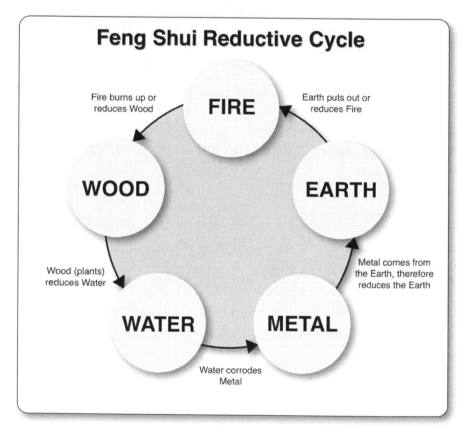

Figure 19

At one of my seminars, a man shared how he began to understand why he was always feeling worn out around his wife and two daughters. He was a Yin Wood type who, according to the **Productive Cycle**, was supporting and expanding the Fire types. His wife and two daughters all charted as Fire elements. According to the **Reductive Cycle**, Fire reduces Wood. He realized he needed to spend more time being around his element of Wood, and doing more activities where he could get recharged from water, the element that recharges wood. I encourage you to realize you are choosing your situations and are not a victim of people who are drawing energy from you. For numerous reasons, you create situations that allow you to demonstrate who you are. It is always perfect until it no longer serves you.

This man who was a Wood Trigram demonstrated his desire to support and uplift his wife and daughters by his attraction of three Fire types. Perhaps his belief behind this attraction was that he had to sacrifice himself in order to demonstrate his love. His new awareness from Feng Shui resulted in his own self-nurturing by taking more camping trips in the woods where he would be connected to his own element, and scheduling more fishing trips to be near water, the element that uplifts him. Some people like to help others, and they create lots of relationships where they are always giving. If they do not recharge themselves with the element that supports them through people of that Trigram or activities around those elements in nature, they will get very tired and resentment could build up.

Each person has a different element that is reductive to their own element. Time does not allow us to run around and chart everyone before we form relationships. The solution is that it is imperative we know ourselves. Feng Shui can help us be aware so we can choose people and elements in nature that help to recharge and uplift us.

I refer to the **Dominant Cycle**, illustrated by *Figure 20*, as the Transformation Cycle because when anything is dominated, it will change or transform. In the case of nature some elements dominate others naturally. This is not a good or bad thing, it just exists, it just "is." Earth dominates Water. We see this in the example of sandbags filled with earth helping to change the direction water flows, often preventing flooding. Water dominates Fire. When water is used to put out fire, transformation results and homes and lives are saved. Fire melts Metal and causes metal to be transformed into functional items as well as beautiful works of art, such as: metal sculptures, frames and bodies for automobiles, and metal chairs. Metal dominates Wood allowing an artist to carve creative pieces of art out of wood, or allowing a carpenter to transform wood, providing lumber to build a home. Wood (as in trees and plants) dominates Earth as we see a tree with its roots digging deep to draw nutrients from the soil.

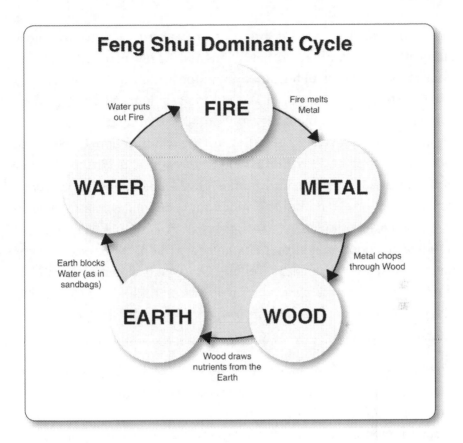

Figure 20

One example of this cycle is when a Wood personal Trigram, according to the **Dominant Cycle**, is dominant to a person with an Earth personal Trigram. This relationship is often a gift, which helps the Earth Type to become a stronger person, as often happens when a person must choose to run away, or to stand up for themselves and speak their own truth without sacrificing the relationship.

The **Dominant Cycle Chart**, *Figure 20*, illustrates those elements that dominate other elements. For example: a Metal house type, which is determined by its position on the land, would have a stronger impact on a Wood type resident, as illustrated by this chart with the metaphor of Metal chopping through wood. Metal dominates Wood according to the Domination Cycle. The same occurs for an Earth in a Wood type home, a Fire in a Water home, and a Metal in a Fire home. It all made sense to me each time I analyzed a building and found an occupant who struggled in their career, health, and/or relationships. I found that whenever the building type dominated that challenged person, it became a major factor and my first concern. Telling someone it would be helpful to them to move was often met with resistance. Embracing change is a big part of our resistance to moving forward and supporting our own personal innate qualities.

I had a client who was married to the same woman for over twenty years and was a caring father of a son and daughter. The father couldn't keep a job, which put great stress on the family. Even though his wife had a good career, she was considering a divorce because of his lack of contribution to the finances. I charted the wife and children and they were all East Group types. When I charted the husband, I found he was a West group type, but the house was an East type and supported the wife and kids. The house did not support the husband or his career, no matter how hard he tried.

When he and his family realized his only concern was for his family over the concerns for himself, they saw him in a whole different perspective. As the supportive person, he had chosen a home, without knowing it consciously, that supported his family instead of himself. The man's primary thought   to do whatever it took to support his family led to this situation. He didn't realize that the Universe just says, "OK," and they purchased a home that supported everyone but the father.

When you check the Personal Trigrams of each person in your household or business, according to the **Productive, Dominant, or Reductive Cycles**, you will begin to see how each is supported, or not, by the energy type of the building. **Chapter 7** explains in detail how to determine your building's Trigram (Element) and its East West Group sitting type.

The **Dominant Cycle** is described by one element dominating another and transforming it, for example: when water is used to put out fire, it results in the protection of lives and structures. Often the event we perceive to be "bad" turns out to be quite a blessing. Relationships within the **Dominant Cycle** can be a gift for both people.

When a parent is dominated by their child, it tends to be difficult for that parent to establish boundaries and discipline their child. This type of relationship teaches the parent about boundaries and discipline. Even though it can be a difficult relationship for the one being dominated, especially if they are the parent of a child who dominates, it causes the one being dominated to become stronger. I believe we ask for spiritual growth in certain areas before we are born, and that is why we have come together in certain relationships in order to achieve our own personal growth. We can blame those who dominate us, or we can become aware and change who we are to improve that relationship. We always have choices, even though sometimes we think we do not, due to the limitations we put on our thinking. In the spiritual thought of Zen, it is stated that the Spiritual Warrior's battle is always with the self.

To bring about balance in a dominant relationship, we bring in the element between the two, according to the **Productive Cycle**. By looking at the **Productive Cycle**, *Figure 18* and seeing what element is missing between the two elements, we can introduce the missing element and bring about balance. Fire dominates Metal (the Fire element in nature is used to melt Metal). When we bring in the Earth element, it will reduce Fire, based on the **Reductive Cycle**, *Figure 19*, and it will strengthen Metal based on the **Productive Cycle**, thus the relationship comes into balance and creates harmony. The Earth element can be brought into the relationship in a variety of ways: with Earth type people, sometimes an Earth child for a married couple, through nature as in rocks and mountains, through the house Trigram being Earth, and through the furniture, accessories, or architectural background materials such as stone, marble, and porcelain, depending on the interior energy captured when the home was built, which I will discuss in **Chapter 11** of this book, and in my *Do It Yourself Feng Shui Guide.*

In Feng Shui, as in life, we can count on things always changing. Nothing remains the same. Letting go is the most important action one can take to bring in abundance, and is often one of the most difficult things for my clients to understand. When we hold on to something, it occupies space and time, and therefore, we do not allow room for more to come in. Time and again in client consultations, one of the biggest obstacles for them in moving forward is letting go. This "letting go" may come in the form of a career change, a separation of a friend or a business associate, a child getting married or going off to college, or a family moving from their home.

This study of the cycles of nature helps us better understand our relationships and how we have contributed to them and attracted them. By applying the remedies suggested from the Productive chart in your life and relationships, you can help improve your life. You cannot change the actions of those you are interacting with. Sometimes they will choose to continue to be in a dominant, or a reductive relationship, even though you have decided to change your behavior to enjoy a more productive relationship. When you do this, you will see more productive relationships come into your life, and fewer dominating or reductive types. Because you are seeking balance, do not be surprised that when you change the way you are responding to someone, that person replaces you with a friend/partner who plays the role you used to play so they can continue to dominate or reduce. We all change in own time based on what we are here to experience.

I often see people, who have gone through a divorce or who feel they do not have control over their own life, create relationships they can dominate in order to feel in control during a time that feels very out of control for them. That relationship may be represented by a friendship, an element of nature they feel powerful around, or the actual Trigram of the house where they live, or the building where they work. Supporting the need to take back their power in a positive way is very important to their healing.

We are all creating our own reality in every moment. Many times our desires are sabotaged by our inner fears. Those inner fears are usually based on the fear of loss, fear of letting someone down, be it yourself, your child, or your parent, or of letting go. I feel that at one time or another we have all experienced a form of loss that has caused us great pain. Instead of accepting that pain as part of life, part of the Yin and Yang that all things are always changing, we attempt to prevent the pain or loss from ever happening again. What we resist persists, and we continue to bring more fear, pain, and self-sabotage to us. Our desires become faded dreams.

Fear stops the natural flow of energy. When we are operating from fear, our whole body tightens up and prepares to defend. Some are always in this state of preparedness, therefore blocking the natural flow of energy through the body. Our society has become one of fear, of being on constant alert, which gives way to a heightened supersensitive awareness that can be good since people are waking up and noticing what is around them. We are discovering the magical energy around us that is always creating naturally. We start to notice how synchronicities begin to happen.

When we remain aware, choosing what feels best to us without the concern for money or love, always choosing unconditionally, and at the same time relax, trust, and allow time for events to occur, this magical energy begins to flow naturally. Some refer to this phenomenon as being in "The Zone"; I like to call it "being in the flow." The key is to trust and allow, accepting the outcomes as always perfect from the more intelligent force that is creating with us in every moment. We create ourselves anew in every moment based upon our choices. Holding onto the past will not keep things from changing. Because relationships are what most of us value so dearly, I find they are the hardest and most painful to let go.

The creative field of energy has no judgment; anything we desire can be created. Our world is a gift to experience who we are. The creative energy around and within all of us is referred to by some as God, and the Universe by others, operating directly in connection with our thoughts or prayers. Your environment or God is not causing your delays, poverty, and hardships. The thoughts you choose about who you tell yourself you are, attracts that energy to you to support your idea about yourself. Until you are ready to change your idea about yourself, you will remain in a business, home, or with people who continue to help you see who you are choosing to be. If living in a state of fear, many people live their lives full of thoughts that reinforce how hard life is for them. Once you become clear about improving your life, people and events appear to support you. Feng Shui remedies work faster when the person is ready to receive the results Feng Shui can bring!

Letting go can be even more challenging if you have created a co-dependent or dominant relationship. You will know you are in a co-dependent relationship when you cannot stop thinking of someone when you are apart, and when you are attached to the results of their activities. Many parents are co-dependent, especially mothers who have created co-dependent relationships with their children. Avoiding decisions in one's own life by focusing on the child allows the parent to live through the child, never having to make life-altering decisions. Basically, it is safe. Often couples will have a parent-child relationship where one can make all the decisions for the other, or one may choose to live vicariously through the other's activities.

When you study the cycles of nature in Feng Shui, you will learn a lot about yourself and the relationships you are creating. Co-dependent relationships tend to be those where one person dominates and another allows it. The dominant/transformation cycle is one to study closely if you feel you are in a co-dependent or dominant relationship. One behaves like a victim and the other like a rescuer, always being there to "save the day," thus feeling they have a purpose in life.

We are all seeking love and attention. Some have learned to do it in an independent, self-reliant way, others in a "poor me" helpless way. The poor me type will usually seek someone to tell them what to do and constantly instructing them what to do next. This behavior allows them to avoid being blamed for making the wrong decision. The independent, self-reliant, sometimes controlling person will often team up with those wanting directions so they can tell them what to do and continue to feel in control. Keeping the balance is the challenge and the goal to creating peace and harmony in your life and in your relationships.

Many who cannot find joy in just being, playing, or celebrating life create co-dependent relationships in order to feel needed as a rescuer, or to feel as a victim that there will always be someone they can lean on. Often both partners have a fear of letting go of the familiar roles they have often played since childhood. They have confused these actions as expressions of love. The victim will create a situation of helplessness or illness to see how many people love him and come to his rescue. The rescuer uses the victim in order to "save the day" and to demonstrate their love.

People have often asked why God doesn't step in when times are tough and instantly change things for the better. I believe God does not need to demonstrate love by being a rescuer. God is that creative force of life energy all around us, allowing each of us to figure out for ourselves what we desire, which demonstrates total unconditional love, and is the reason our experiences, especially those we call mistakes, are so important to our journey. Allowing ourselves and our children to fail often results in great wisdom! The Universe is set up for us to find our own answers, and when we do find our own answers, the feeling is joy!

Asking the Universe for help puts that energy into motion. Those who pray testify it is powerful. Many of us find asking for help a form of weakness. The more emotional the asking, the faster the energy moves to bring the desire into reality. Religious leaders have taught that Jesus never healed anyone until they asked because he saw the perfection in each moment. If we do not like who we have become, then we may choose again. By choosing what we don't want, we are able to see better what we do want. Life is about choices. Yin and Yang comes into balance as both partners in a relationship stop playing the roles of victim and rescuer, which results in happier and healthier relationships and lifestyles without guilt or resentment.

Our homes and work environments are a reflection of how we feel. What we choose to put in our environment says a lot about who we are. Many people are becoming proactive instead of reactive concerning their own health and lifestyle. Feng Shui is based on an awareness of how our environment affects us. The five elements, as I have outlined above, have been used in Feng Shui and Chinese medicine throughout history. When these elements work together, balance occurs in our world.

Feng Shui is the study of nature and how it impacts people. Studies have indicated that people who live in the mountains tend to be stubborn, and people who live near the water are considered clever and swift!

The **Productive Cycle** is critical to the practice of Feng Shui. Understanding this cycle, and your Personal Trigram in relation to your location on the **Productive Chart** is important. Studying it will help you become more aware in making choices which support you, and result in a feeling of security and well-being.

To have health and abundance, you must desire it first, believe you can have it, and be able to accept it when it comes to you. Many desire it but when they get it cannot keep it because they feel they did not deserve it or didn't work hard enough to earn it. Many have been taught they do not have the right to even ask. I once made a joking comment to someone who was waiting in my car while I went into the post office. I said, "I will ask God to provide a short line so you won't have to wait long for me." He replied, "You can't ask God for that." No one had ever given me a list of what I could and could not ask God for! Many people never ask for help because they have been told, "You can't ask God for that!" And they believe it!

I have found when I discover certain energy in a home and give people a solution to help change the energy, they will sometimes not follow the advice. In one such case I was hired by a realtor to help change the energy in her client's home in order to help sell the home quickly. When I returned, the items had not been rearranged, and the fountain was not running, as I had suggested. The owner's husband told me his wife was afraid the fountain would catch fire while she was away from home. This same woman did not consider unplugging the refrigerator or other appliances, only the items that could change the energy and move her forward. It seemed obvious she was sabotaging the change of energy around her. If her house sold, she had told me confidentially, there would be a divorce from her husband and she didn't want that to occur. She was sabotaging moving forward with her actions, and blaming it on something else. We all do this, often never realizing that is what we are doing.

Usually, when someone blames something on events or situations or even people, it is to avoid their own true feelings about that situation. Unfortunate events that appear to be accidents often are really self-sabotaging occurrences by people who cannot share the truth about their feelings and desires. Things appear to be happening to them because they haven't given themselves permission to choose something of which others might not approve, thus avoiding being criticized by others, or disappointing someone.

When a client got clear on what he wanted for a career, jobs and opportunities came in rapidly for him. He attempted to take a position in the entertainment field, in the same industry as his father. As a Wood Yin Trigram, working on computers (the Fire element) came easily to him. Being quite creative, a natural trait of the Wood-Yin Trigrams, enabled him to receive a good wage with full benefits at a very stable company. As time progressed he started getting to work late. The hours were not rigid, and yet he was tardy. He and his employer agreed the situation was not working.

Losing that job gave him an opportunity to take a job he had long desired working outdoors driving trucks, which made him independent, and truly in his element as "The Traveler." He took a cut in pay and worked long hours, but I saw a great deal of joy when he told me about his new career. When we follow our hearts and our passions instead of the money and the prestige of the position, we create magic and our lives become exciting.

There are many ways to change the energy in a space once a person realizes they want things to be different. Awareness and a desire to change are essential, along with having the courage to ignore what others will think. "Do just once what others say you can't do, and you will never pay attention to their limitations again." Edmund Brown, Jr.

For the most part, when a Feng Shui consultant brings in certain colors for the environment, it is with the intention and purpose to create a change in energy, in turn affecting the life of the user of that space. Solid colors of medium intensity are used to get quick and definite results. That doesn't mean pastels are not good for interiors, but medium or high intensity colors change the balance of the energy of an interior and are very effective Feng Shui remedies. You will know when the color brings about a balance in the energy of a room because the chosen color will feel good in that space. When changing my client's environment by moving objects and accessories to different areas, I immediately feel a shift in energy and so does my client!

When we bring a color into our environment, it is as if we are bringing in one of the five elements: Fire, Earth, Metal, Water, or Wood. Each color vibrates at a different rate. When red or its compatible colors of maroon, burgundy, or purple, which represent the Fire element of nature, are brought into an environment, the energy intensifies. The colors yellow, tan, and beige represent the Earth element, similar in tones to those colors found in the earth. A person of the Earth Trigram will find themselves comfortable with these colors in interiors without realizing why. The element of Metal is represented by white and gold, Water by blue and black, like the blue ocean or a deep well full of water with its dark black essence. The color that represents the Wood element is green, as we see in the leaves of plants, trees, and grass.

In **Chapter 6**, I discuss each element in detail, referring to the **Eight Personal Trigrams**. We gravitate toward the element that matches our personal Trigram. My friend, Julie, loves to play tennis. She started years ago when rackets were made of wood. Since her personal Trigram in Feng Shui is Wood Yang, it makes sense she would want to be outdoors around the trees, holding a wooden racket. Wood dominates the Earth element so she would be powerful on a cement court, which is the Earth element, taking her power back and feeling strong.

Feet and throat are the parts of the body that relate most to the Wood Yang Type Trigram. She is good at tennis, which requires quick use of her feet. If she were out of balance, throat and feet might give her more problems. A characteristic of the Wood Yang type is Yang energy. Yang is outgoing, energetic and expanding. The symbol for the Wood Yang is Thunder, which is quick and fast. Quick and fast movements are very important in tennis.

Wood in the Productive Cycle of nature supports Fire. Julie has always been a good cook and seems to enjoy being around fire, whether it is the kitchen cook top or the outside barbecue. The Wood element thrives around water, and Julie has always enjoyed participation in water sports and boating with her family over the years. The Productive Chart helps illustrate why the elements of Fire and Water have always played a prominent role in her life, as they are adjacent to the Wood element.

Chapter Six

The Eight Personality Types: How to Better Understand, Connect, Persuade, Sell, & Lead Them

Personal Trigrams can be used to help you get in touch with that part of you which may have been forgotten. You will either resonate with your personal Trigram, or you may say that does not match who I know myself to be. You may want to ask yourself, "Am I being who others want me to be, or am I honoring myself?" People react with surprise at how their personal Trigram seems to fit. It is so accurate that the leaders of China have been selected using this principle, and couples are matched for marriage based on it.

As a leader, one of the greatest benefits derived from having a deeper understanding of the eight Feng Shui Personality types is to help you identify the strengths of your team. Studies have shown that when people are working from their strengths, they have a greater passion for their work, they perform their job with greater ease, and they are more productive and contribute greater value to the team. Use this system to bring together your team and you will enjoy a happy and productive team with greater harmony and success.

First chart all the people on the team according to their year of birth. Remember, anyone born before February 5th will be charted according to the previous year. Use *Figures 2 through 5* in **Chapter 1** to calculate each. For example, January 1949 would be listed in the year 1948 and would be an Earth Yang type. Take a minute to gather and chart all the birthdates of those you are leading.

Now that you have the birthdates, make a note of what each type is best at. Earth Yins make great managers because they need to nurture and support others. When they manage they are patient. The Earth Yang must be involved in doing something creative. They work well as part of a team as long as their creative ideas are acknowledged and used. They enjoy the variety of working with lots of different people and activities. The Metal Yang must lead, manage, supervise and be in- charge. They work best independently. The Metal Yin has the ability to bring humor and fun to team activities. They may be quiet due to their yin energy, but they make good communicators, and want to bring play and fun to the workplace.

I heard a story about an employee named Mark who worked on a construction team. Each morning Mark met with his fellow workers, chatted with them and told jokes. During football season, Mark would organize a football pool and share some highlights of the game and announce the winner of the pool the morning after the game. Then a new supervisor was hired to manage the construction team. This new manager decided to fire Mark. He felt Mark was wasting time and never getting anything done. He looked at Mark as a distraction.

Shortly after, the productivity of the team began to drop. The new manager decided to interview his employees to ask what they felt was the reason for the reduction in productivity. To his surprise each told how much they looked forward to coming to work each day because Mark made their job more fun. Don't underestimate the power of the Metal Yin to uplift your company and produce a positive outcome.

Water Yins are diplomats. Being yin energy they will go around a problem to get the job done while avoiding conflict. They are great negotiators and bring people together. The Wood Yang type is a great business confidant. You can have them help make good decisions, which will benefit your business. They are secretive, kind and generous, and able to quickly organize and set-up meetings and training events as they think on their feet. Wood Yins are fixers and must travel. They may move from site to site on location doing problem solving activities or travel on behalf of the company. The Fire Yang is a workaholic. When a Fire Yang is passionate about what they are doing and given responsibility, they will come in early, stay late and work overtime to get the job done. They are great at explaining and teaching and are good to orient and teach various jobs and company policies to a new hire.

Be sure to look at the compatibility between people when forming partnerships or joint ventures in business projects. Fires support Earths, Earths support Metals, Metals support Waters, Waters support Woods, and Woods support Fires. The more challenging partnership would be a Water working with a Fire. By bringing in the person of the element between the two—in this example of Water and Fire, the missing element is Wood, yin or yang—the relationship and the team flows. Always remember to bring in the missing element between two elements using the **Productive Cycle Chart** to pair people for productivity and compatibility.

In each of the **Eight Personal Trigrams** listed in this chapter, I discuss the colors and the body parts related to each, the elements that support, reduce, and dominate, and the tendencies that are unique to each type. Note that the body part for each type is their strongest part of the body and is also the part of the body most often affected when a person is stressed.

The Earth Element – Yin: This Trigram is supported by Fire and is known as "mother earth," the element that most relates to all the other elements. They tend to be quite nurturing, almost to an extreme, hence the nickname, "mother hen." Earth Yin is seen in occupations that use their nurturing characteristics: nurses, physical therapists, counselors, realtors, and other types of service-related careers.

Often they will be found working with their element as bricklayers, sculptors, china painters, gardeners. Earth types are often found working in the garden; it grounds them and recharges their "mother earth" nature.

Body parts related to the "Mother Earth" Trigram are the abdomen or stomach, which relates to the area an expectant mother carries and nurtures her child before giving birth. You will often see the Earth-Yin type with stomach problems due to worry. Because of their Yin qualities, as discussed in the previous chapter on Yin and Yang, they tend to be more sensitive and take in not only positive energy but also negative energy from those around them. Learning to separate themselves from the feelings of those around them is very important to their own health. Fire replenishes according to the **Productive Cycle**, and water helps them feel strong and powerful based on the **Dominant Cycle Chart.** Their symbol is earth. Refer to *Figure 21* for best facing directions and *Figure 22* for best sleeping directions.

Figure 21

Figure 22

The Earth Element – Yang: This type person is outgoing and energetic due to their Yang qualities and tends to be one of the most creative of the Trigrams. You will often find them in occupations that involve lots of interaction with people. It is hard for them to sit at a desk for more than two hours at a time. They dislike repetition because of their creative nature, but office work is fine if limited and if they have enough variety in activities and with people. They invent new ways of doing things and see the bigger picture, which may not always include attention to details. They can bring people and things together in a fun, unusual way, leading them to creativity in the field of design, fashion, film, and architecture. Since they enjoy being around lots of people, a career in sales works well for them. Don't expect this creative Earth to be happy sitting in a classroom all day unless it is a photography, art, or music class, which utilizes their creativity. They tend to be stubborn because mountain is their symbol. The body parts associated with this Trigram are those that remind us of a mountain: knees, elbows, and the vertebrae, which may cause them problems if they are out of balance from too much stress. You will find them happiest if they live near the mountains or can see mountains in the distance. Fire replenishes them and water helps them feel strong and powerful. Refer to *Figure 23* for best facing directions and *Figure 24* for best sleeping directions.

Both the Yin and the Yang Earth elements are supported by Fire, showing up in their work in the form of computers, electrical engineering, electricity, lighting, cooking, and barbecues. Fire shows up in their environments by a longing for fireplaces, warm climates, and the colors red, maroon, burgundy, or purple.

The Earth Yin and Yang Trigrams support Metal, therefore they can also be found working with metal, or using metal as tools. They enjoy numerous activities: from working with metal equipment in gyms, car and plane repair, metal bodywork, drafting equipment, air conditioning and heating, to travel by train, plane or auto.

They are most comfortable around their own element of Earth, with various stones, clay, or porcelain, for instance, or working as bricklayers, sculptors, china painters, and gardeners. The Earth Trigrams enjoy working in the garden; it grounds them and recharges them when working with their own element. Earth, as seen in nature, dominates Water. Earth Trigrams will often bring in the element of water in their environment or gravitate to water when they feel stressed and out of balance in order to feel more in control.

Earth Trigrams will gravitate toward the colors yellow, tan, and beige, which relate to the earth, and the supportive Fire colors: burgundy, maroon, or purple. They will also gravitate toward Metal or the colors white and gold because they, in turn, support Metal. Metal will have a tendency to slow the earth person down, or drain them when in large doses, as we see in nature, when Metal is removed from the Earth, it reduces the Earth of its minerals. Studying the cycles of nature in the previous chapters will help these factors become clearer.

The two Earth types, Yin and Yang, get along well together because they are the same element. When one is Yin and the other is the opposite Yang, they form a whole together. I refer to these types of relationships as gifts because they bring balance to the relationship. Recommended bed sheet colors for an Earth Trigram are: maroon, burgundy, purple, red, rose, yellow, tan, or beige. Earth types are dominated by Wood, and relationships with Woods can be more challenging. A Wood will always win over Earth when it is something that is important to the Wood.

Sitting For Earth Yang

Best Facing Direction in Order

#1 best = SW
2nd best = NW
3rd best = W
4th best = NE

Best Direction to be facing while seated. 1st direction Southwest is most alert.

Figure 23

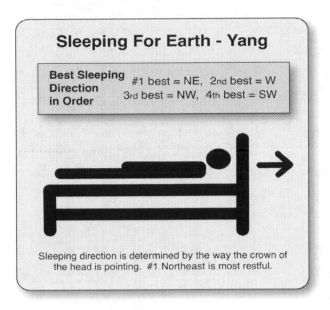

Sleeping For Earth - Yang

Best Sleeping Direction in Order	#1 best = NE, 2nd best = W 3rd best = NW, 4th best = SW

Sleeping direction is determined by the way the crown of the head is pointing. #1 Northeast is most restful.

Figure 24

The Metal Element – Yin: This Trigram is supported by Earth. Metal Yins tend to be quite fun loving, teaching us all how to play. They have a good sense of humor, earning them the nickname, "party animal." After overcoming the fear of speaking in front of an audience, they tend to excel in presentations and public speaking, always spicing their talks with humor. They are seen in a variety of occupations, often involving the element of Metal related to travel and having to do with cars, trains, or planes.

Frank Lloyd Wright, born June 8, 1867, was a Metal Yin Trigram, and he was supported by earth as depicted on the Productive Cycle. No wonder he incorporated stone, the Earth element, in all his buildings by using bricks and cement. As Metal is the parent of Water, he also incorporated water in the Falling Waters home. In

Southern California, his Hollyhock House uses unique metal lighting fixtures. Because Metal dominates Wood, it is no accident he used beautiful woods throughout his homes by custom designing the wooden seating and furnishings.

Colors relating to Metal types are white and gold. Since they are dominated by Fire, Metals might choose to be around Fire less with the exception being when they are surrounded by the elements of Earth, Metal, Wood and Water. Refer to **Figure 25** for best facing directions and **Figure 26** for best sleeping directions.

I determined a woman in one of my classes to be of the Metal Yin Trigram. As I described her desire to plan parties, I asked if she had many parties in her home with friends, or entertained her husband's business associates. "No, never, and the idea of working with metal serving trays and planning parties does not fit me," she declared. On further probing, she confessed she did own a catering service at one time!

The mouth region is the body part related to the Metal Yin. They may grind their teeth or have problems in the mouth area if they are out of balance. Because the mouth is related to their Trigram, the Metal Yin may be a public speaker in the field of sales or marketing, or work in the field of dentistry. They love to travel, which makes sales a great occupation for them. Because of their Yin qualities, as discussed in the previous chapter on Yin and Yang, they tend to be more sensitive and take in not only positive energy, but also negative energy from those around them. Learning to separate themselves from the opinions and feelings of those around them is very important to their own health. The symbol related to the Metal Yin type is marsh.

When we sold our home in the Santa Monica Mountains, it was purchased by a woman who matched the home, and she loved it. I was not surprised; when I did her Feng Shui Trigram, she was a perfect match for the house. The house Trigram was a Metal Yin and that was her personal Trigram as well. When the house matches the person, much support occurs for that occupant and studies have shown that the match brings the potential for the occupant to experience peace and good management. In addition, Metal, according to the Productive Cycle, is supported by Earth; the natural landscape around the home in the Santa Monica Mountains.

Sitting for Metal - Yin

Best Facing Direction in Order

#1 best = NW
2nd best = SW
3rd best = NE
4th best = W

Best Direction to be facing while seated. 1st direction NW is most alert.

Figure 25

Sleeping for Metal - Yin

Best Sleeping Direction in Order	#1 best = W, 2nd best = NE 3rd best = SW, 4th best = NW

Best sleeping direction for the crown of the head.
1st direction W is most restful.

Figure 26

The Metal Element - Yang: This is the most powerful Trigram in Feng Shui. All the past leaders of China have been born under the Metal Yang Trigram. When women were born under this sign in China, they were often considered too powerful, and went unrecognized since women were not to hold places of power in China. In their long history, there were only two Empresses I know of. This Trigram is considered one of power and authority, and is associated with the head of the household, or the head of a business. Often people of this Trigram will be put in charge of leadership positions. If they are not given a position of power, they will often create their own position within a company or start their own business in order to gain desired power and control, so natural to their personal Metal Yang Trigram. They tend to be very competitive people. I spoke at a meeting of interior designers, and the Metal Yang person in the group admitted she was elected president of the group only one month after joining the organization!

When I charted Tara Lipinski, the Olympic Gold Medal Ice Skater, who participated in the 1998 Winter Olympics, I found her personal Trigram to be that of a Metal Yang. I was fascinated that she was skating on her element of Metal when she won her Gold Medal. The Metal element is the "parent of Water" and she certainly was powerful over water, skating on ice! Since Metal types are supported by the Earth element, like mountains, and the 1998 Olympics was held in mountainous Nagano, Japan, those factors were supportive and important to her success. Add to that the competitive nature and determination of a Metal Yang and it's no surprise she won the Gold!

The body parts associated with the Metal Yang are the head and chest. Often, under stress this Trigram will experience headaches, migraines, or lung and/or chest problems relating to breathing. With the head being associated with this Trigram, it is easy to see the reason for their desire to "head up" their own company or department. Heaven is the symbol of the Metal Yang, leading many to become airplane pilots, or leaders in church. This Trigram supports the element of Water. Since lungs are a strong part of the body, Metal Yang types are known to be excellent swimmers. The Metal element supports the Water element, and their competitive nature causes them to lead or win. Refer to **Figure 27** for best facing directions and **Figure 28** for best sleeping directions.

The Metal Trigrams, both Yin and Yang, are comfortable around their own element of Metal, using metal as tools, and able to work indoors in offices with metal desks and metal cabinets, or travel in cars and planes. They will be found in all sorts of activities from working with metal equipment, exercising in gyms and car and plane repair, to doing metal bodywork. Since the element of Metal supports the element of Water, these Metal Trigrams are also seen doing work as hairdressers who use metal scissors, as skin divers serving in the Coast Guard, as lifeguards, firefighters, or in other job-related activities around metal and/or water.

If the Metal-Yang Trigram is working as a hairdresser, they will usually end up owning the shop as they fulfill their desire to lead. Hobbies or sports-related activities for these Metal types revolve around Metal and Water such as: boating, jet skiing, or travel on cruise ships and airplanes. The Metal draws its support from the mountain or Earth where minerals can be found. To recharge, they will often go hiking in the mountains, rock climbing, or enjoy gardening. Women will tend to lean toward acquiring metal jewelry. Often I find this Trigram working to sell or create custom jewelry. Their environment will often be quite clean, filled with metal furniture or accessories. Recommended bed sheet colors for a Metal Trigram are the colors of the earth element: yellow, tan, and beige, and the colors of the Metal element: gold and white. Green is also fine for bed sheets, a color this Trigram dominates.

In nature the Metal element dominates the Wood element. The Metal Trigrams, when feeling out of control, will bring wood into their lives in the form of trees, plants, wood furniture, or people of the Wood Trigram in order to feel more in control. I have a friend of the Metal Yin Trigram going through a divorce, and during that time I noticed he first acquired a Bonsai tree for his desk in his office. Then he took up guitar lessons. The guitar brought in the element of Wood and had metal strings. He moved to a new home and added lots of new wood furniture. By bringing more of the Wood element into his life, he was taking back his power after a distressing divorce that had been initiated by his wife. We surround ourselves naturally with the elements of nature to bring us comfort and relaxation, support, and provide feelings of empowerment when we desire to be uplifted.

Sitting For Metal - Yang

Best Facing Direction in Order

#1 best = W
2nd best = NE
3rd best = SW
4th best = NW

Best Direction to be facing while seated. 1st direction West is most alert.

Figure 27

Sleeping For Metal - Yang

Best Sleeping Direction in Order	#1 best = NW, 2nd best = SW 3rd best = NE, 4th best = W

Sleeping direction is determined by the way the crown of the head is pointing. #1 Northeast is most restful.

Figure 28

The Water Element - Yin: The Water, being Yin only, has no Yang and is directly opposite the fire element, which is Yang only in its energy type. Those with the Water element as their personal Trigram tend to be great diplomats and negotiators, always knowing the best thing to say in the moment. They tend to flow like water, going around conflict, as water flows around rocks and other blockages. Being the Yin type, they will demonstrate a calm energy, desiring more quiet time, more inward energy, and are quite sensitive to nature. Due to their Yin nature, they tend to wait rather than reach out to resolve problems.

Their work and play activities often revolve around their personal element, Water. Because they nurture plants, they are often seen to have a green thumb and have the greenest and healthiest lawn on the block. Metal supports them so they will be comfortable working or vacationing on cruise ships surrounded by water. Water types thrive when participating in water sports: jet skiing, or boating, as well as working out at the gym several times a week, which actually recharges them.

The strong body parts related to Water Yins are blood and water. Water Yin children have ear infections, or challenges related to the fluids of the body. When Water types become stressed, they will have challenges with blood or fluids in their body. The symbol for Water types is water. Their interiors will be furnished with colors of Water: blues, blacks, or the color of Metal, their supportive element: white or gold. Their environments will be clean and decorated with pictures of water and accessories of metal. The preferred color of sheets for a good night's sleep is blue or black, the colors of Water, and white or gold, the colors of Metal. Sheets in the colors of fire, like reds and maroons, are also fine since these colors represent the fire element, which this Trigram dominates, resulting in a feeling of power for them. Refer to **Figure 29** for best facing directions and **Figure 30** for best sleeping directions.

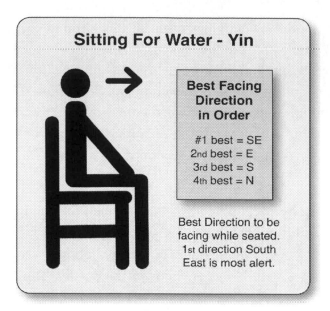

Figure 29

Figure 30

The Wood Element – Yin: This Trigram, supported by Water, is known as "the traveler." They tend to be quite sensitive, often having psychic ability, which helps to make them highly creative people. They are seen in many different types of occupations where they provide service to others. Because of their desire to travel, they think on the move. Traveling, driving in a car, plane, train, ship, or walking allows their minds to find clarity. Body parts related to the Wood Yin are thighs and buttocks, which relate to the trunk of a tree. Strength in the thighs makes them good at track and field, water polo, volleyball, soccer, tennis, and any sport that depends on their upper legs and buttocks. Because they are "the travelers" and their symbol is the wind, it is not surprising to find women or men of this Trigram involved in car racing. In their youth they are often known to acquire more tickets for speeding, which is related to their passion for travel. This element is quite healthy and because the symbol is the wind, their biggest health concern would be minor and may only be rheumatoid arthritis.

Often they will be found working with their element, in the outdoors around trees and green plants. The Wood element in nature is considered to be the parent of Fire, therefore they are found in occupations where Fire is prominent, such as firefighters, in electrical engineering, (computers being a fire element), and lighting design. They are dominant over the Earth element, making them wonderful archeologists, traveling to faraway places. As hobbies, they are often playing computer games or inventing something using electrical tools because of their highly creative mind. It grounds and recharges them to be in or near Water (often taking two showers per day), surfing, snorkeling, scuba diving, swimming, or participating in any other water sports. Occupations relating to water support them, such as: lifeguard, Coast Guard, or careers in the Navy.   The color that relates to the Wood Yin is green. Refer to *Figure 31* for best facing directions and *Figure 32* for best sleeping directions.

Because of their Yin qualities, as discussed in the previous chapter on Yin and Yang, they tend to be more sensitive and take in not only positive energy, but also negative energy from those around them. Learning to separate themselves from the feelings of those around them is very important to their own health. This could also be why Wood Yins tend to take two showers a day, or relax in the spa or tub especially in order to relieve stress.

Figure 31

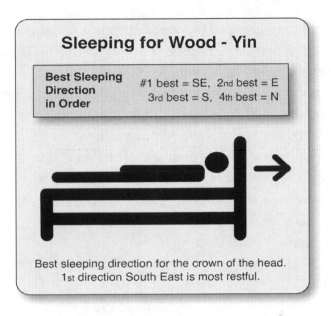

Sleeping for Wood - Yin

Best Sleeping Direction in Order	#1 best = SE, 2nd best = E 3rd best = S, 4th best = N

Best sleeping direction for the crown of the head.
1st direction South East is most restful.

Figure 32

The Wood Element – Yang: This type person is outgoing and energetic due to their Yang qualities. Their symbol is Thunder, causing them to get upset quickly and just as quickly get over it. The body parts associated with this Trigram are feet and throat, parts of the body that make the most noise, which is related to their symbol of Thunder. Their work is often related to being on their feet a lot. They voice their opinion and make good speakers and teachers since the throat is associated with the Wood Yang Trigram. When they are out of balance, their feet or throat may give them problems. They are kind, generous, and tend to be quite secretive, which makes them great business confidants. They are happiest living near lush green plants and water. Refer to *Figure 33* for best facing directions and *Figure 34* for best sleeping directions. **Both the Yin and Yang Woods** are associated with Wood elements and are supported by Water. Pictures of nature with water scenes are often seen in their homes and offices. The Yin and Yang Woods are supported by the element of Fire, which shows up in their work and play in the form of computers, electrical engineering, lighting, cooking, and barbecues. They love to have Wood in their environments from natural wood floors to wood furniture, lush green plants, and the color of their element, green. Fire shows up in their environments by their craving for fireplaces, warm climates, and the colors red, maroon, burgundy, or purple. Fire tends to reduce wood and has the tendency to relax this Trigram, or drain it if fire is in excess.

Because Wood dominates Earth, these types would be comfortable around cement, mountains, and people of the Earth Trigram. When they feel their life is out of control, they may be drawn to the Earth element or Earth type people to get back a feeling of power. To create a more positive supportive sleep environment, the recommended colors for bed sheets are green, representing the Wood element, and blues or blacks, representing the element of Water. The colors of the Earth element: yellow, tan, and beige give them a feeling of power.

Fire will have a tendency to slow down the Wood type or drain them in large doses, as we see in nature when forest fires occur and reduce the trees in its path. To become clear about how people interact with each other using the elements, familiarize yourself with the cycles of nature and the Yin and Yang theory referred to in the previous chapters.

The two Woods: Yin and Yang, get along well together because they are of the same element; since one is Yin and the other is Yang, they come together to form a complete circle with their opposite. As the relationship matures, it can be quite a gift, bringing balance to each person. By observing your partner or friend, you can learn how to expand in the area of Yin or Yang. Each brings something different to the relationship in order to teach the other how to achieve balance within.

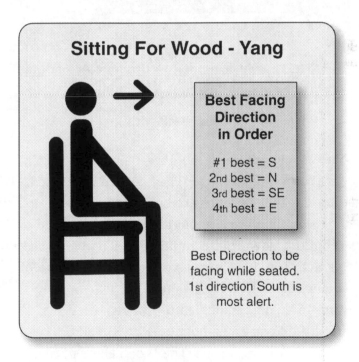

Figure 33

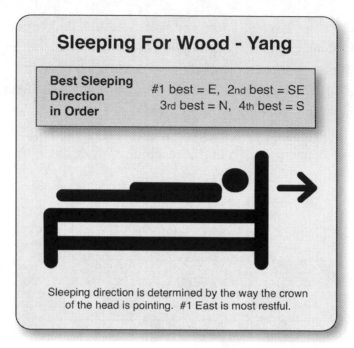

Figure 34

Fire – Yang: Those with the Fire element as their personal Trigram tend to be workaholics. They go and go. Parents of these children often say they never run out of energy. Since water, as seen in nature, puts out fire, the element of Water can be used to slow the Fire type children down quite rapidly. Bath before bedtime and other water activities tend to relax this Trigram. One of my Fire Trigram clients shared how it now made sense to her why she would always want to light candles immediately after her shower to recharge herself. Wood gives them energy, like adding a log to a fire and watching it burn vigorously. The Wood element comes in many forms: trees, green grass, wood furniture, wood floors, office paperwork, magazines, books, and the color green. This type enjoys nature walks among trees and plants.

People of the Fire element love to have a fireplace, and often want one in every room of their home, since fire is their symbol. They enjoy a good burning fire, a barbecue, or sitting in front of a campfire. They would also enjoy the fireworks on the 4th of July. Their color is in the Fire tones: red, burgundy, maroon, and purple. You may find these colors selected for their interiors, along with the color green representing the element wood, as well as the element of earth and/or its colors of yellow, tan, and beige. Wood supports fire.

In nature the Fire element supports Earth. Fire is considered "the parent of Earth," causing them to enjoy gardening, hiking among rocks, or selecting stone, brick or pottery for their homes. They are most compatible with another Fire Trigram, or the Wood or Earth Trigram. They are usually good cooks and do very well with computers. Computers are considered a Fire element due to its high level of electricity. Often I find a Fire Trigram with red hair! There is only one Fire, and that is Yang energy.

The Fire element dominates Metal. Fire melts metal, causing it to be transformed often into something quite beautiful. Because of the Fire tendency to feel dominant around Metal, they will be comfortable indoors around metal desks and file cabinets, in vehicles of metal such as planes, trains, cars, or ships. Fire Types are supported by wood, trees and plants, and outdoor activities will be important to them.

The body parts associated with Fires are eyes and heart. This Trigram may fall in love a lot or require eyeglasses at an early age. When experiencing stress in their life, those with the personal Trigram of Fire may find body parts relating to the eyes or heart being most affected. This type is often a passionate reader. "We see their heart through their eyes," has often been said of a Fire person.

Recommended bed sheet colors for a Fire Trigram are green, maroon, burgundy, purple, red, or rose, the colors of Fire. Green, the color of the Wood element is also good for sleep. White and gold, the colors of the element of Metal, which is dominated by Fire, works for bed sheets also, and these colors give Fires a feeling of power. Refer to *Figure 35* for best facing directions and *Figure 36* for best sleeping directions.

Figure 35

Figure 36

Chapter Summary - Eight Personal Trigrams:

WEST *Group Personal Trigrams:*

Earth Yin – West Group – (NE, W, NW, SW)

Element:	Soft Earth
Yin/Yang:	Yin
Tendencies:	Very caring, nurturing, "mother hen"
	Tends to worry about others before self.
Symbol:	Earth (relating to "mother earth")
Body Parts:	Abdomen, or Stomach
Supported by:	Fire (colors of fire – red, purple, burgundy, maroon)
Colors(s):	Yellow, Tan, Beige
Earth Supports:	Metal
Number:	2 – Mother
Orientation:	Southwest

Earth Yang – West Group – (SW, NW, W, NE)

Element:	Hard Earth
Yin/Yang:	Yang
Tendencies:	Very creative, enjoys variety & people,
	Tends to be stubborn
Symbol:	Mountain
Body Parts:	Bony parts, knees, elbows, vertebrae
Supported by:	Fire (colors of fire – red, purple, burgundy, maroon)
Colors(s):	Yellow, Tan, Beige
Earth Supports:	Metal
Number:	8 – Youngest son
Orientation:	Northeast

Metal Yin – West Group – (NW, SW, NE, W)

Element: Soft Metal
Yin/Yang: Yin
Tendencies: Fun loving, good communicator, good in sales,
                referred to as the "party animal"
Symbol: Marsh
Body Parts: Mouth, chest, and teeth
Supported by: Earth
Colors(s):   Gold, White
Metal Supports:Water
Number: 7 – Youngest daughter
Orientation: West

Metal Yang – West Group –(W, NE, SW, NW)

Element: Hard Metal
Yin/Yang: Yang
Tendencies: Head of company, head of household, leader
Symbol: Heaven
Body Parts: Head and lungs
Supported by: Earth
Colors(s):   Gold, White
Metal Supports: Water
Number: 6 – Father
Orientation: Northwest

EAST Group Personal Trigrams:

Water Yin – East Group –(SE, E, S, N)

Element: Water
Yin/Yang: Yin
Tendencies: Diplomat, peacemaker, great negotiator, avoids conflict
Symbol: Water
Body Parts: Ears, blood, and kidneys (fluids in the body)
Supported by: Metal
Colors(s):   Blue, Black
Water Supports:Wood,
Number: 1 – Middle son
Orientation: North

Wood Yang – East Group –(S, N, SE, E)

Element: Wood
Yin/Yang: Yang
Tendencies: Secretive, kind, generous, tends to be explosive
Symbol: Thunder
Body Parts: Throat and feet
Supported by: Water
Colors(s):   Green
Wood Supports: Fire
Number: 3 – Oldest son
Orientation: East

Wood Yin – East Group –(N, S, E, SE)

Element: Wood
Yin/Yang: Yin
Tendencies: Restless, called "The Traveler" quiet, sensitive,
                  and intuitive
Symbol: The Wind
Body Parts: Thighs, and buttocks, which relates to a tree truck
Supported by: Water
Colors(s):   Green
Wood Supports: Fire
Number: 4 – Oldest daughter
Orientation: Southeast

Fire Yang – East Group –(E, SE, N, S)

Element: Wood
Yin/Yang: Yang
Tendencies: Determination, drive, workaholic, great teacher
Symbol: Fire
Body Parts: Eyes, and heart ("See their heart through their eyes")
Supported by: Wood
Colors(s):   Red, Burgundy, Maroon, and Purple
Fire Supports: Earth
Number: 9 – Middle daughter
Orientation: South

Chapter Seven

Understand East vs West Group Personalities & Buildings to Simplify Taking Your Life & Career to the Top

When I consult with a client, the first thing I must know is the individual Trigram of each occupant of the building, whether in a home or business. I look for compatibility between the building and the person or persons occupying it. I want to first see if they have selected a place to work or live that generally supports them in an East or West Group building. I also look for relationships between the people who live and work within that environment.

A building, like a person, falls under one of the **Eight Trigrams/Five Elements** listed in **Chapter 6**. After determining the Element Type of a building: Earth, Metal, Water, Wood, or Fire, I can help my client determine if the building type is compatible with each occupant in the building, whether it's a home or an office. When a home is not a supportive match to their East or West Group Type, it is important to place the bed direction in one of the most supportive directions for their sleep. For anyone being compromised by an unsupportive house type make sure their sleeping directions are supportive to their personal element type. Our bodies heal and recharge at night while we sleep so setting the bed direction to the individual is important.

In an office or workspace when the building is not a match to the individual's East/West Group Type, then it is important to make sure their facing direction is good as illustrated in **Chapter 6**.

Illustrations of interior floor plans within a building for supportive sleep and supportive work spaces are discussed in **Chapters 9 and 10.**

To determine if a building is supportive to its occupants, you must begin by interviewing the individuals occupying the building. According to their year of birth, determine their personal Trigram by element and East/West Group Type. The **Productive Cycle Chart** in **Chapter 1**, *Figure 1* shows which Trigrams are East Group and which ones are West Group Types. It will be helpful to know your East/ West Group type when reading through this chapter.

If you have a floor plan of your building, it will help you understand your building's sitting and facing direction. Otherwise, study the floor plan illustrations in this chapter as I explain how to determine your own building type. The first step is to look at the overall floor plan of the building to determine which way the building sits and faces. Do not be confused by the entry door, which may be placed along one side of the building, and not necessarily in the expected location at the front near the street.

The East or West Group Type is determined by the sitting position of the building. To tell which side of the building is the sitting, think of a building like a giant armchair. When seated, our spine is positioned against the seat or back of the chair. It is the place in the chair that gives support to the body. To determine the sitting side of the house, compare the spine of the body to the support of the various rooms within the home, and look for those areas that provide the most support. The kitchen gives us support with a food prep area to help provide us with nourishment. The bathrooms are where we have space to cleanse and groom to support our bodies. Our bedrooms provide a place to sleep and rest so that our bodies and minds are able to recharge. These places in a home are usually private areas and because of that are often placed in or near the back of the house to provide us with support. The backyard is usually in the sitting side of the house away from public view near the kitchen, bath, or bedrooms.

In a business, the kitchen areas, marketing and accounting departments, and storage spaces are more private and are usually placed toward the back of the business, whether it is a hair salon, restaurant, or commercial building. These spaces would be considered to be at the back of the building, and in Feng Shui referred to as the sitting side of the building.

The facing part of the house is always opposite the sitting part of the house, like a person sitting in a chair, the front of the body is opposite the vertebrae of our back. In this facing direction, we address people, speak and converse openly, and make public contact. The house facing direction is the part of the house used to greet friends, the public areas where guests enter, the living room, dining room, and the home office, which is usually placed close to the front door. The street is usually in the front, on the facing side of the house, but there are exceptions to this.

Exceptions to the above descriptions are homes with panoramic views from the backyard, such as the homes on the Pacific Coast Highway in California. The kitchen is in the front near the street, representing the support side, the back, or vertebrae side of the house. The living room is opposite the kitchen, usually on the beach and ocean side, representing the facing and viewing area that opens out to a public area. It is usually accessible to receiving the public from the beach side, in contrast to other homes with a front open to a street or sidewalk, also accessible to the public.

The kitchen location, no matter how great a view it has, is the most important factor in determining the sitting of a house. Kitchens on the street side in front of the home, often next to a front door, for instance, indicate the sitting side of the home, as illustrated in **Figures 37** and **38**. The front door and street are not considered in determining the sitting direction. The garage is excluded from our energy grid because it is not considered livable space, open and flowing to the rest of the living areas of the house, and is usually closed off by a fire door and fire wall protecting the interior part of the home from its energy. With the large garage door constantly opening and closing, the garage is unable to hold energy for long compared to a home with smaller door and window openings.

The Following Floor plans illustrate sitting and facing directions:

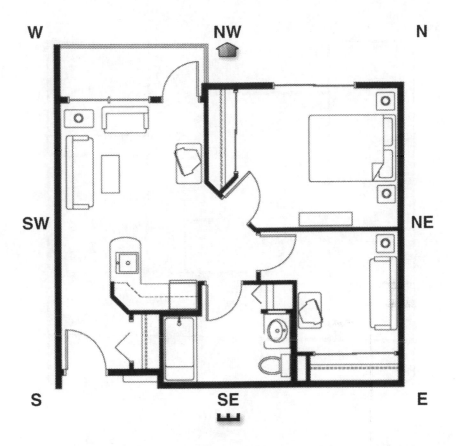

Figure 37

Figure 37 illustrates the sitting in the Southeast and facing direction in the Northwest. This could be a dorm room or apartment. The sitting direction is located on the kitchen/bathroom side opposite the view. The sitting location in a large apartment complex will often be located in the hallway between units inside the building. The facing direction usually has more windows than the sitting side. **This is an East Group, Wood Yin Type home with a Southeast sitting. Note:** the front door does NOT determine the facing or sitting direction.

Figure 38

Figure 38 illustrates a similar layout as *Figure 37* having the living room with view windows opposite the sitting direction, entry, and kitchen. The kitchen determines the sitting of this home close to North side front door entry. This is an **East Group, Water Yin Type home with a North sitting**. **Note:** the front door does NOT determine the facing or sitting direction.

The next illustration is a more common home with the kitchen and bath and bedroom toward the back yard. Most traditional homes are built with a front door near the living room where guests are welcomed.

Figure 39

Figure 39 above illustrates a typical home with living room and front door next to each other facing East. The kitchen is on the back side of the house off the backyard.   The kitchen determines the sitting.   The sitting is opposite the living room and view. **This is a West Group, Metal Yin Type home with a West sitting. Note:** Remember the house type is determined by the sitting position and NOT the facing or the front door.

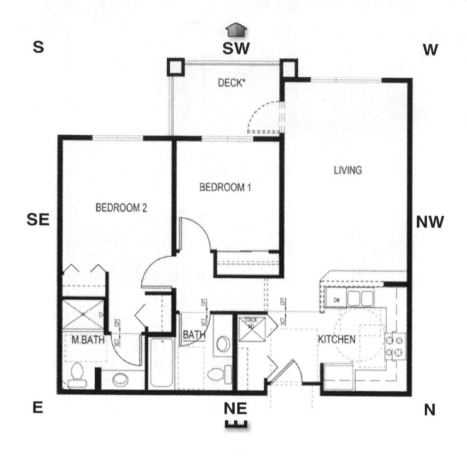

Figure 40

Figure 40 illustrates a **Northeast sitting, West Group, Earth Type Building**. Notice the support areas of the Master Bath, Hall Bath, and Kitchen are all on the sitting side of this home. This example could be a single family home, an apartment or a condo. Notice the front door is located next to the kitchen on the sitting side of the home.

Figure 41 illustrates the **Eight Trigrams and their Corresponding Directions**. This is an ancient diagram where all the numbers in a row add up to 15 when added up horizontally, vertically, or diagonally. This is also called *The Magic Square*, discussed in detail in my **Do It Yourself Feng Shui Guide**. This diagram shows all of the elements and the directions and numbers which determine each building types. This diagram has been referred to as The Magic Square and For example, Fire is associated with the South direction and the number 9. A building that has a South sitting is referred to as a Fire East Group Type Building. A Northwest Sitting building is associated with the Metal Yang element, number 6, and is a West Group Type Building.

NINE QUADRANTS
Eight Trigrams and their Corresponding Directions

SE	S	SW
Wood (Yin) 4	Fire (Yang) 9	Earth (Yin) 2
E	Center	W
Wood (Yang) 3	Earth 5	Metal (Yin) 7
NE	N	NW
Earth (Yang) 8	Water (Yin) 1	Metal (Yang) 6

Figure 41

Determining your building's sitting and facing directions:

Determining the sitting and facing direction of a home or business is critical for an accurate analysis of the environment. Many very experienced Feng Shui consultants have been known to misinterpret the sitting and facing of a building, causing chaos to occur in the environment when remedies are placed in incorrect areas.

To help you determine your building's sitting and facing direction, refer to the residential floor plan examples in *Figures 37, 38, 39, and 40* which will help you understand how different residential buildings sit and face. In commercial buildings it is simple to tell the front, or facing side, of a building and the back, or sitting side, of a building because the facing is the obvious place to receive clients or customers.

The exception is when a commercial building faces strongly in one direction with a bank of windows, but has an entrance along the side of the building. Look for the elements that determine the sitting. No view, parking lot, few windows, and no signage on the back side of the building are usually indicative of the sitting. The facing is always opposite the sitting direction. Remember the sitting direction determines the building's *East/West Group Type*. Refer to the East Group/West Group Building Types in *Figures 42 and 43*.

These 4 buildings are best for East Group Type Trigram People.

East Group Buildings			
SITTING DIRECTION	**FACING DIRECTION**	**ELEMENT TYPE**	**YIN or YANG**
North	South	Water	Yin
East	West	Wood	Yang
Southeast	Northwest	Wood	Yin
South	North	Fire	Yang

Figure 42

Note: the sitting directions determine the building type.

These 4 buildings are best for West Group Type Trigram People

West Group Buildings			
SITTING DIRECTION	**FACING DIRECTION**	**ELEMENT TYPE**	**YIN or YANG**
Southwest	Northeast	Earth	Yin
Northeast	Southwest	Earth	Yang
West	East	Metal	Yin
Northwest	Southeast	Metal	Yang

Figure 43

Once you have determined the sitting direction, it is time to take a compass reading. I use a Chinese compass called a Lopan. Taking a reading from the building's sitting direction using the Lopan helps me determine the building's Element, and its East or West Group type. The specific degrees on the compass help me determine the energy captured in the building when it was built, the yearly visiting energy, and the monthly energies. For example, a south sitting building would be a Fire East Group Type. The building's Trigram Fire Element, which is part of the East Group type when we refer to the Productive Cycle. To keep things simple, you can use a regular compass for hiking and camping to determine your building type. If you can obtain the exact degrees on the compass, you can access a more comprehensive reading of the building's energy blueprint, which is covered in my *Do It Yourself Feng Shui Guide.*

Some of my clients have used a compass on their smart phone, and I have seen discrepancies from the actual Chinese Lopan. I'm told it's because some have set their compass on true north and magnetic north would be the better choice. I recommend using a Lopan, GPS, or actual camping compass to determine the sitting direction. If possible, check with someone who owns a Chinese Lo-pan to insure you are getting the magnetic north reading.

Listed below is a review of the steps to be taken to determine your building type:

1. Interview each person in the building to determine their Element, Yin/Yang, and East or West Group type based on their year of birth using the chart in **Chapter 1,** *Figures 2 through 5*. Remember, if their birth date is before February 5, use the previous year.

2. Draw a simple floor plan or sketch of the building to scale.

3. Determine from your floor plan the sitting direction for the building. (Refer to the paragraph on *Determining your building's sitting and facing directions* following *Figure 41*. You will find it helpful to review the floor plan examples *Figures 37 through 40* to best determine the sitting direction.)

4. Stand with your back to the sitting direction and face in the opposite direction toward the facing of the building, usually out the front door toward the street.

5. Make note of the degrees on the compass that point toward the sitting direction behind you.

6. Once you know the direction of the building's sitting, you can determine its Element, East/West Group type and energy within. The East Group Building Chart *Figure 42* and the West Group Building Chart *Figure 43* in this chapter will help you confirm the building type according to its sitting direction.

In 1998 as I used our home in the Santa Monica Mountains as a case study to learn Feng Shui, I became aware that a very critical energy was coming into our home for that year. According to the compass reading, the house was a reverse house: it was not good for people or money. All combinations, from the sitting position on the land to the energy in each bedroom, to the energy which came into the entrance and into the heart (center) of the house, seemed to reinforce the energy of delays, struggles and pain. I am thankful it was a West Group house: it supported my husband and me. As a result, we were both able to make the best decisions for our family. This example will make more sense to you when you learn about the permanent energy in a building, covered in my next book *A Do It Yourself Feng Shui Guide*.

Based on the sitting direction of your compass reading, and the East and West Group Building Charts, you will be able to see if you are a match to your building type. See if your Personal Trigram obtained from the Birth Chart in **Chapter 1** falls into the same *East or West Group Type* as your house, or office by referring to **The Productive Cycle Chart**, *Figure 1,* and the *East/West*

Building Types listed in ***Figures 42*** and ***43*** on the previous pages.

There is no one house that is perfect for everyone. We each have different likes and dislikes, goals and destinies that are unique to us; buildings have energy unique to them as well. The clearer you become on the choices for your own specific personal life goals, the easier it is to select a home or business with the potential to best support that specific goal. See the house examples in ***Figure 44*** to select a home that is supportive to your Personal Trigram Type and life goal. The Chart, ***Figure 44***, shows a Water type person has the highest potential to achieve Good Fortune and Great Fame when they live in a SE sitting building: referred to as an East Group Wood Yin Building Type. For a Fire type to achieve Good Fortune and Great Fame, they would be best in an East sitting building referred to as an East Group Wood Yang Building Type.

For a Metal Yang, the potential for the same outcome of Good Fortune and Great Fame would be highest if they lived in a West Sitting, West Group Metal Yin home. This was the case for my son, a Metal Yang Trigram, who achieved a Junior National Level in swimming during his senior year of high school, breaking the school swim record and was awarded a full swim scholarship to a university, when he lived in our West sitting home in the Santa Monica Mountains. From my own experience, it seems the **East/West Group Building Theory** is more important than the energy within the building, although I remember the energy in my son's room was also very positive.

Each Trigram is shown in this chart in ***Figure 44*** to have four types of buildings that bring them the most success, and the four types of buildings that have the potential for the most challenges. Find your personal Element Yin or Yang Type on the following chart. The top four building types listed by sitting and facing directions under your element type have the highest potential to be the most supportive for you.

Building Interpretations for Each Trigram

Interpretations	EARTH Yin		EARTH Yang		METAL Yin		METAL Yang		WATER Yin		WOOD Yin		WOOD Yang		FIRE Yang	
	Sits	Faces	Sits	Faces	Sits	Faces	Sits	Faces	Sits	Faces	Sits	Faces	Sits	Faces	Sits	Faces
1. Great Fortune and Fame	NE	SW	SW	NE	NW	SE	W	E	SE	NW	N	S	S	N	E	W
2. Wealth and Supportive Friendships	W	E	NW	SE	SW	NE	NE	SW	E	W	S	N	N	S	SE	NW
3. Harmonious Family Life and Good Public Relations	NW	SE	W	E	NE	SW	SW	NE	S	N	E	W	SE	NW	N	S
4. Peace and Successful Management	SW	NE	NE	SW	W	E	NW	SE	N	S	SE	NW	E	W	S	N
5. Potential for Arguing and Lawsuits	E	W	S	N	N	S	SE	NW	W	E	NW	SE	SW	NE	NE	SW
6. Challenges and Possible Misfortunes	S	N	E	W	SE	NW	N	S	NW	SE	W	E	NE	SW	SW	NE
7. Harmful Influences, Accidents, and Disasters	SE	NW	N	S	S	N	E	W	NE	SW	SW	NE	NW	SE	W	E
8. Career Difficulties, Financial Challanges, Robbery	N	S	SE	NW	E	W	S	N	SW	NE	NE	SW	W	E	NW	SE

Figure 44

Finding the best house type or commercial space and moving in may not be as simple as it sounds. When a person works from within to personally grow and change, they start to attract the energy that matches their energy within. A person cannot live in a building that has the potential to bring them peace unless they desire peace and are willing to be peaceful. Having peace within ourselves first will draw to us the energy of a building that has the potential to attain peace and harmony. "Like energy" attracts "like energy." That is why it is so important to get clear about what you truly want, then believe and trust it comes to you.

You cannot be in a situation that doesn't match your inner self for very long without feeling unhappy, confused, or stressed. This situation occurs when our inner spirit does not vibrate with the same energy, goals, or desires of others, or that of the building, and eventually one will change or fade away. When people are changing spiritually and growing within, they may notice friends, family or partners drift away and/or change their behavior. As they grow, transitions occur in their career, as well as in their home location, bringing in new opportunities, people, and experiences.

When you study your home, see how your Personal Trigram matches with the House Trigram and how the other members in your family fit as well. See if one or more members are of the East Group type, and the others of the West Group or vice versa. Based on the results you want to occur in your life, refer to the **Building Interpretations Chart** illustrated in *Figure 44* to find the building type to support you in achieving the results you seek.

There are two things that cannot be changed without costly remodeling of a home. The first is the East and West Group type house based on the house's sitting position on the land illustrated in

Figures 48 and 49. The second is the energy of the letters A, B, C, D, E, F, G, and H defined later in this chapter. The placement of these letters for each of the eight house types (Wood yin, yang, Water yin, Fire yang, Earth yin, yang, and Metal yin, yang) are illustrated in **Figures 45 through 52.** This energy is created when the building's foundation is placed on the site; based on the sitting position, you can determine where these energies fall.

Letters of the Building and their Energy Interpretations:

Figures 51 through 58 illustrate Eight Building Types, according to their Sitting Positions referencing the letter interpretations.

Note that the advanced interior energy of the house has not been included in this analysis. The permanent energy captured when the building was built is represented by the mathematical numbers. This energy is discussed in my next book; **Do It Yourself Feng Shui Guide**, showing how the energy has a stronger effect on individuals than the letters. Often, the permanent energy captured when the building was built may be very good for wealth or health and can override the E, F, G, H energy, which is not as favorable.

To discover the interior permanent energy captured when the home was built, you will need to take an accurate compass reading to determine specific degrees on the compass for the sitting direction specific to the building. For the most accurate information, retain an experienced Feng Shui Consultant who uses a Chinese compass.

The letters of a building are permanent and cannot be altered without major renovation. Select the grid from **Figures 46 through 53** which corresponds to your building type and place it over your drafted floor plan, matching each box with its proper house direction. See where the letters fall for your specific building.

Draw a grid over each floor of the building plan, adjusting the grid to the building's floor plan footprint as I have illustrated in the sample in **Figure 45**. Each floor of the building may be slightly different in shape and will need to have the grid adjusted to that floor plan size.

The A, B, C, D areas are the best ones in the building (home or business), and these areas should be used for: entrances, bedrooms or office areas where the occupant spends most of his time, or often enters and exits through these spaces. If this energy is not favorable, and remodeling is not possible, the client may opt to move to another location, depending on the advanced energy reading of the mathematical numbers in combination with the letters.

A = Most favorable and has the potential to bring huge fortunes, great respect, and the opportunity to be a pillar in the community!

B = This energy has the potential to maintain good health and safety to its occupants.

C = This energy has the potential to create a harmonious marital relationship or early marriage and is also good for fortune.

D = This energy has the potential to provide occupants with peace and good management.

E = This energy may give adverse effects such as money loss, lawsuits, and arguments.

F = This energy is related to having the potential for failed relationships, and arguments.

G = This energy is related to abandonment by all friends, relatives, and or business associates. Also relates to possible fires and accidents. When the "G" is seen in combination with other energies, the potential to acquire huge and quick fortunes is possible. This information takes a skilled Feng Shui person to determine and requires a compass reading on site.

H = This energy is associated with having a potential for accidents, robberies, incurable diseases, or an unproductive career.

Avoid taking these letters literally. Many factors influence how a skilled Feng Shui consultant would factor in this information.

Note: It is most desirable to enter a building, and sleep in an A, B, C. or D area.

The illustration in **Figure 45** is a good example of having the letter B energy located at the front door quadrant, here in the South. The potential for huge fortune is shown by the letter A, located in the bedroom in the North corner.

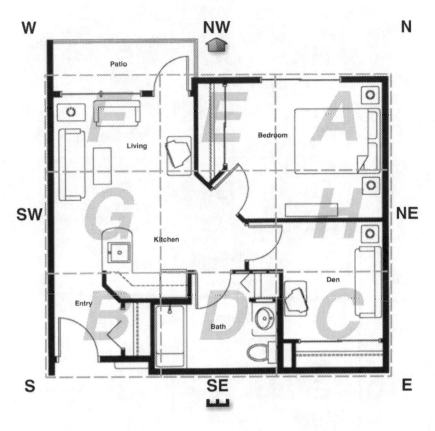

Figure 45

Figure 45 shows you how to place the letters on your building floor plan after you have divided the floor plan into 9 equal boxes. This illustration takes the floor plan illustrated in **Figure 37** and adds the letters for the SE sitting home shown in **Figure 53**. **Figures 46 through 53** show the specific letter placement for each house type. To locate the letters for your building be sure to refer to the sitting direction of the building.

121

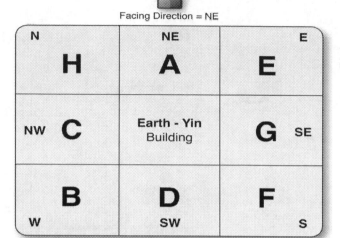

Facing Direction = NE

N	NE	E
H	**A**	**E**
NW **C**	**Earth - Yin** Building	**G** SE
B	**D**	**F**
W	SW	S

Sitting Direction = SW, Earth - Yin

Figure 46

Facing Direction = SW

S	SW	W
E	**A**	**C**
SE **H**	**Earth - Yang** Building	**B** NW
F	**D**	**G**
E	NE	N

Sitting Direction = NE, Earth - Yang

Figure 47

Facing Direction = E

NE **C**	E **H**	SE **F**
N **E**	**Metal - Yin** Building	**G** S
A NW	**D** W	**B** SW

Sitting Direction = W, Metal - Yin

Figure 48

Facing Direction = SE

E **G**	SE **E**	S **H**
NE **B**	**Metal Yang** Building	**C** SW
F N	**D** NW	**A** W

Sitting Direction = NW, Metal Yang

Figure 49

Facing Direction = S

SE	S	SW
A	**C**	**H**
E **B**	**Water - Yin** Building	**E** W
G	**D**	**F**
NE	N	NW

Sitting Direction = N, Water - Yin

Figure 50

Facing Direction = W

SW	W	NW
E	**H**	**G**
S **A**	**Wood - Yang** Building	**B** N
C	**D**	**F**
SE	E	NE

Sitting Direction = E, Wood - Yang

Figure 51

Facing Direction = NW

W **F**	NW **E**	N **A**
SW **G**	**Wood - Yin** Building	**H** NE
B S	**D** SE	**C** E

Sitting Direction = SE, Wood - Yin

Figure 52

Facing Direction = N

NW **H**	N **C**	NE **E**
W **G**	**Fire - Yang** Building	**A** E
F SW	**D** S	**B** SE

Sitting Direction = S, Fire - Yang

Figure 53

Chapter Eight

Create a Residential Space that Positions You in Power & Ensures Your Good Health, Sound Sleep, & Prosperity

Having years of formal education in design and architecture, and experience applying what I had learned, once I found Feng Shui I cannot imagine ever again designing without first considering the information about the people and their space according to the principles of Traditional Feng Shui.

Residential spaces that create relaxation & reduce stress:

Color has a big impact on people within a space. High contrast of colors used in the interior causes more energy because, as your eye moves around the interior of a room, the eye stops at every change of color. We call this the rhythm of the room. Color contributes to this rhythm. Every time you change colors within the space, your eye stops, which is very disruptive to creating a calm environment.

A more peaceful environment results when architectural background, walls, ceilings and floors are painted the same color. A calm and more spacious feeling is achieved when wrought iron railings of a staircase are painted to match the interior wall behind it. Inexpensive bookcases and cabinets are best when they match the wall color since your eye will focus on the more important accessories and artwork and the background disappears. Often, I see the furniture color competing with the accessories, which causes a very busy, stressful feeling within a space. By using only three colors in a room, the visual appearance of the space becomes calmer and relaxes the eye, especially if one of the colors is a neutral beige, tan, soft white, or soft gray.

When selecting color use the darkest color for the floor, a shade or two lighter for the walls, and a light shade of the wall color for the ceiling. Avoid white ceilings that cause your eye to stop at the top of the wall color which creates the illusion that the room is unfinished.

Lighting:

Lighting is very important in a home. Keep windows clear of overgrown plants. Replacing older metal windows with energy saving vinyl windows brings a clean, bright uplifting feeling to a home, and prevents leaking energy. Energy can be changed in a dark entry or windowless bathroom by adding a skylight or recessed lighting. Solar tubes can be easily applied to a one-story house to bring daylight to a dark hallway. It brightens an area so well I have been tempted to look for the light switch!

Floor Plans:

The physical layout of a home is very important. Today, in our Western culture, home developers give greater thought to the placement of staircases. When designing a home, avoid placing a staircase directly in front of a doorway or exit; the energy from upstairs then flows down the stairs and exits directly out the front door. Homes with front doors in direct alignment with the back door experience energy coming in and going out too fast. When remodeling is not an option, placing art sculptures, interior French doors, or plants between the two doors will help slow down the energy. There's a greater potential for arguing in homes with angled walls. Slanted as well as beamed ceilings cause interruptions in airflow, and heavy beams create neck or headaches for the person sitting below. In some homes it is difficult to place furniture to avoid the beams. If headaches occur, the homeowner may consider adding a flat false ceiling to conceal the beams.

The wife of a real estate broker/developer contacted me to help her with the challenges the whole family was experiencing related to the energy of career delays and struggles, represented by the mathematical numbers 9-5 in the center of their 4,000 sq. ft. home. To remedy the 5, which is earth energy, Metal is needed. The **Reductive Cycle Chart**, *Figure 19,* shows that metal is the remedy to reduce earth. The family moved a 300-pound bronze angel from their entry hall to the center of the home where metal was needed. Every day the family passed by the angel and touched her wings; their gestures became a very uplifting remedy that soon brought financial gains for them. The mother later told me her teenage daughter's acupuncture doctor noticed a change in her patient. "Your house must have improved energy," the Chinese doctor commented. She had not been told about my Feng Shui reading and remedies.

Bedrooms:

Beams above a bed can cause sleeping problems, and if the beam runs directly above the center of the bed running between a couple, that couple can have issues of separation. As mentioned, slanted ceilings and angled walls can cause arguing, but using drywall or fabric stretched from wall to wall can create a flat surface solution. Avoid four-poster beds because the posts are unsettling to someone who may awake in the middle of the night. The posts give the illusion of someone standing next to the bed. Electric equipment, like alarm clocks or light fixtures, are best placed at least three feet away from the head of the sleeper. Since EMF weakens the body and can interrupt sleep, a television, which emits strong EMF energy, is best placed as far away from the sleeper as possible and to the side of the bed instead of at the sleeper's feet. Keeping a TV out of the bedroom is best, and that applies to computers and a work desk. With these distractions in the bedroom, it's more difficult to get away from work for a good rest to recharge the body.

As pictured in the "good bedroom" illustration *Figure 54 (D-2)*, if a closet's sliding doors at the foot of the bed are mirrored, I suggest the mirrors be covered at night with a soft drape for a good night's sleep. In Feng Shui it's believed the spirit travels out of the body at night while sleeping, and when the spirit returns to the body, the mirrors can cause confusion and disrupt sleep.

My client, Susan, recently had the opportunity to move from her corporate office to work from her home. She hired me to do a Feng Shui consultation to help set up her home office and received a lot more information than she expected. She and her husband were having relationship challenges. She was frustrated that he wanted to invest in building his music career instead of contributing to the household income.

When I worked up their report, I found she was a West Group Metal-Yin type and was supported by the West Group Metal Yang house type. Her husband, an East Group Wood Yin type, was not supported by this West Group home, in fact, Metal dominates Wood, which most likely added to his lack of a successful career. In addition, they were sleeping in a bedroom with 5-7 energy, indicating delays and arguing for people. When working with the building's permanent energy, the numbers on the left represent what is affecting people and their relationships. The numbers on the right indicate issues relating to money. This 5-7 also brings a potential for arguing. There was a 9 yearly energy visiting in the bedroom, which indicated the arguing had reached its peak. See **Figures 54 and 55** for illustrations of good and poor bedroom arrangements.

Bedroom Orientations: Good

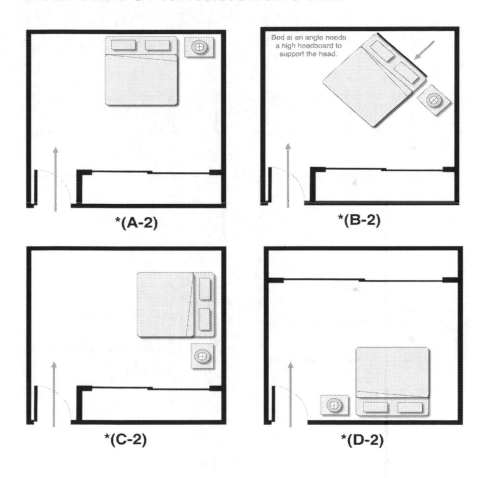

* Protected from energy coming directly in the door.

Figure 54

Bedroom Orientations: Poor

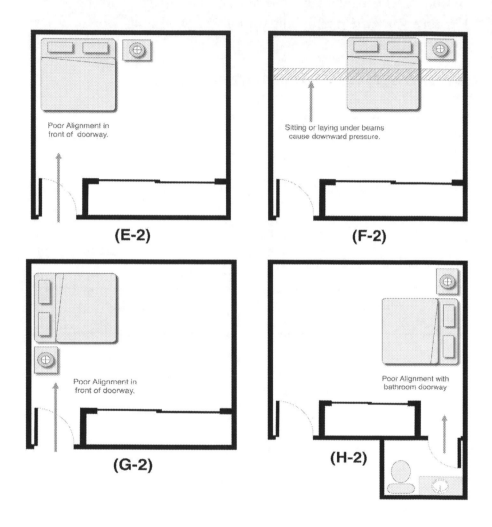

(E-2)

(F-2)

(G-2)

(H-2)

Avoid sleeping in direct line of doorways and avoid sleeping under downward energy from overhead beams.

Figure 55

For Susan and her husband, the center of their home had the same energy as the bedroom, with the numbers 7-5 in a reversed position, indicating the delays were affecting the money earned as the 5 falls on the right side. Again, this challenging energy in the center of the home was having a stronger effect on the husband who was an East Group in a West Group home. The bed direction along with the house type was supporting the wife. Her career was booming and his career was at a standstill.

After reading my report they were both clearer. I always suggest the bed be in the direction of the compromised person, in this case the husband. Sleep is considered one of the most important factors in Feng Shui. With proper sleep, concentration during the day increases, and your energy is higher, two important qualities for career and wealth expansion. It was important to put him in his best sleep direction. I looked for the wealth producing areas of the home to suggest the proper remedies to increase the potential for wealth for both of them. Since they were both working from home, it was also important to have each of their work chair positions in the best direction for concentration. Susan reported back to me that they were much more understanding toward each other. After remedies were placed in the areas with potential for arguing, she noticed the conflicts subsiding; they were both making progress to move forward more easily and were working together to implement changes in the house.

Summary of What to Avoid for Residential Properties:

1. Homes or buildings directly at the end of a cul-de-sac or "T" junction.

2. House or apartment very close to a fire station, police station, or cemetery.

3. Home or apartment below the street.

4. A home on the side of a hill supported by stilts.

5. A home with a street in the front and back of a house.

6. Staircases positioned in front of the front door.

7. Dark entryways.

8. Bedrooms with slanted ceilings, and/or having heavy beams.

9. Home with front door in direct alignment with the back door.

10. Trees or posts directly in front of the front door.

11. Keep windows clear of overgrown plants

Chapter Nine

Tips on Powerful Commercial Spaces: Get More Done, Have Greater Decision Making Power & Authority

Many factors play a part in creating an environment that supports power, authority, and wealth. The most important factor to improve the physical environment at the Office is balance. Balance in lighting is critical and often overlooked: too bright can cause irritability, and too dark can cause depression. Maintaining a balance in temperature helps to keep people alert and focused on the task at hand.

Sitting under a beam or ceiling soffit can cause headaches, as well as difficulty concentrating. Getting rid of clutter, letting go of as many notes, post-its, and excess paper as possible, especially on the workspace and desk surface, allows one to focus on the task with little distraction. By keeping work areas clean, there's less chance for stuck energy, tasks are completed easily, frustration is reduced, and there's an increased feeling of accomplishment. Visualize how you feel when you picture the surface of your desk clean and uncluttered. You will definitely benefit from a cleaner workspace.

I found a good way to clear clutter is to start with the end in mind. If you have lots of paper, stack everything in one pile and remove from your desk. That clean workspace allows you to make decisions easily. Begin with the pile you stacked. Bring only one inch of the pile of paper to your clean desk. Go through the pile putting post-its on each paper. You might label them: to do, file under _____, reading folder, long term projects or the project name. Put the future reading materials in a handy folder you can grab easily when you are off to the dentist, or anywhere you may have to wait and have the time to catch up on your reading. Avoid making folders or doing the filing yourself, it's a job that can be delegated to an assistant.

Avoid Sharp Corners:

I was hired to assist an interior designer with the design of an office for a production company. During the preliminary plans, the designer suggested the client's chair be aligned with his back to a corner structural column, but the client complained, "I feel like I am being stabbed in the back." In Feng Shui the goal is to avoid any corners pointing directly at a person because corners create a feeling of uneasiness, and decrease the ability to focus and concentrate. See illustration *Figure 57*-(G-1) in this chapter for an illustration of this poor Office Orientation.

I suggested that his desk be positioned to give him a full view of anyone entering his office. This example of power and authority has been seen throughout history, demonstrated by many successful leaders. The office of the President of the United States is a perfect example, as he sits behind a desk in full view of two incoming doors to the oval office. The suggestion to place a mirror in front of you when your back is to the door still creates a position of compromise and is not suggested at any time. It is best to avoid positioning a desk where the user sits facing toward a window with the sunlight streaming in on the desk top with white papers causing the sunlight to rebound toward the user's eyes. If you want a view of the outdoors from your desk, turn the desk perpendicular to the window where the light will spill across the desk and not cause a glare when the user is working.

When calculating the advanced permanent energy for the client's office, I suggested the addition of the element of Water to bring about a balance in the energy. The permanent energy analysis, which was derived from advanced math calculations, covered in my *Do It Yourself Feng Shui Guide*, indicated a potential for betrayal, and water was the remedy to help reduce that potential. It was agreed that the sharp-edged column would be rounded and water added to run down the column in a peaceful constant stream.

When the elements of nature are brought inside a building, the occupants often feel an immediate calming effect. When these elements are placed to complement the visiting and permanent energy, determined by a compass reading as in this instance, balance is achieved. Clients frequently report to me there's an immediate difference in the way an environment feels and they feel more comfortable as well. I find those with the personal Trigram of Wood feel much more supported by pictures of water or actual Water elements surrounding them, such as a water fountain, or a fish tank.

Note: The actual remedy of Water or the use of a solid color representing the element is the best remedy. Pictures of water or elements are not a substitute for the actual element or color. Glass is also not considered to be a representative of water in the Traditional Feng Shui Five Element Theory. Elements need to be exposed to the air to be effective, like a fish tank that is open on top. A water cooler or a waterbed have water, which is contained and covered and are not good for adding a water remedy.

Colors:

If colors are dull or depressing, choose cheerful and uplifting colors. A small space with dark wood paneling or dark-colored carpet can be depressing. Use more plants with up-lights to give a feeling of depth to a room and add recessed down lights to the ceiling. Energy is changed quickly in dark corners when lighting is added. Avoid glare because too much light can cause irritability. Remember that colors vibrate at different speeds. Studies were conducted on prisoners to determine how the color red would affect their mood. It was discovered that the color red has a calming effect for the first 20 minutes and then has a negative affect after causing irritability. Be sure to avoid red walls in an office where people are under a lot of stress or need to concentrate on their work. Red is good to imply action and is good for logos and traffic areas to liven up and give people energy. Once again, it is very important to know what the Feng Shui energy is in each area before selecting colors. Unwanted energy, such as delays and sickness, could be increased by using certain colors.

Furniture Placement and Traffic Flow:

Make sure that open shelves are not directly pointed at you when seated at your desk. This creates a strong, piercing energy that disrupts concentration. Avoid placing a desk at the end of a long hallway. Too much energy coming down that hall will cause illness to a person in its direct path. A woman at one of my seminars told me she had developed headaches and flu-like symptoms after she was moved to a desk at the end of a long hallway. When I spoke about a similar situation in my class, she became aware of the cause for her headaches. Previously, her office had been located in a quiet part of the building away from traffic, noise and other distractions. After her move, a great deal of energy was coming directly at her.

It is important to work on the permanent energy analysis, along with the yearly and monthly visiting energies, before selecting furniture placement, a color pallet, and proper elements from the Productive Cycle. Often people choose what supports their personal Trigram. Instead, I encourage them to focus on the building's energy and choose the elements to help balance the permanent and the monthly and yearly visiting energies within the space to derive the most success. Once the environment has been remedied, most people report they feel calmer and happier within the space. See *Figures 56 and 57* for illustrations of good and poor office furniture arrangements.

Office Orientations: Good

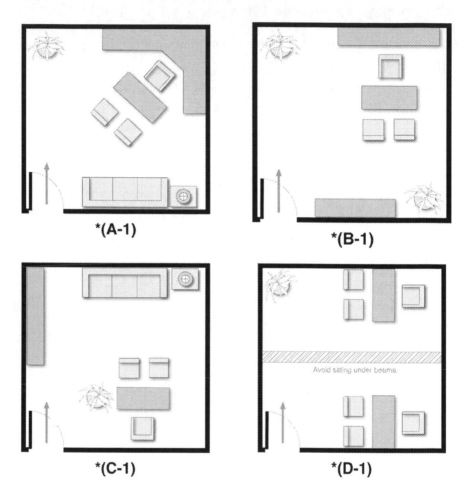

*(A-1)

*(B-1)

*(C-1)

*(D-1)

Avoid sitting under beams.

Furniture placed to protect user from
energy coming in the door.

Figure 56

Office Orientations: Poor

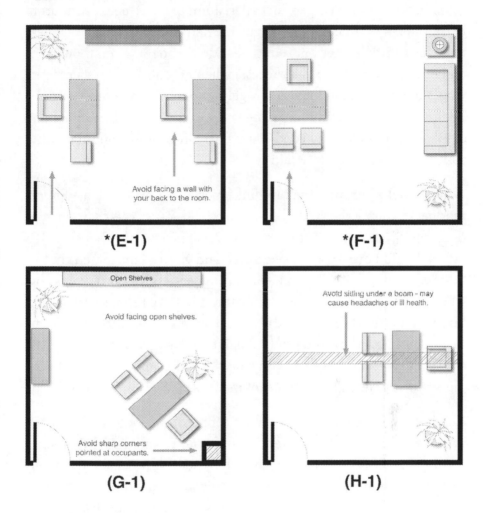

(E-1)

(F-1)

(G-1)

(H-1)

* Avoid sitting directly in front of door, under overhead beam, or having sharp corners pointing directly at you.

Figure 57

Sometimes, when a building doesn't match a client, despite remedies, a major change is in order. John, who owned a restaurant in Hawaii, was a client years ago. He had taken over the business from his retired father but found he didn't enjoy it. Even though the restaurant had once been a success, when he put it up for sale, there were no takers and John was struggling to make ends meet. I did a Feng Shui personality charting on John and his father and discovered John was a Wood-Yang East Group type, and his father was a Metal-Yang West Group type.

When I walked around the building's perimeter and took a compass reading, I found the building was a Metal-Yang West Group type that supported John's father and dominated my Wood client. His father would have experienced peace and good management in this building of the same element as his own personal Trigram. His son, who had been comparing his failures to the father's success, did not understand the building didn't support him, despite his efforts. Because he hadn't wanted to let his father down, John was relieved it wasn't his fault about the business failure, and he admitted he didn't want to be in the restaurant business.

In addition, my analysis showed the center of the building was a 7-5, which meant there was a potential for arguing, and delays on money coming in. John followed all my suggestions to implement many remedies inside and outside the building and within two months he received an offer and completed the sale. His choice to change careers and become a high school drivers' education teacher was perfect for him and brought him much enjoyment, a better match for his Wood Yang qualities such as being kind and generous, able to share information easily, and the ability to think quickly on the spot.

Summary for things to Avoid for Interior Commercial Spaces:

1. Avoid sitting under a beam. (Neck pains and Headaches, plus lack of concentration may occur.)

2. Do not sit with your back aligned with a corner structural column. (Like an arrow pointing at you, it can cause back pain along with uneasy feelings.)

3. Face the door for a position of power. Do not sit with your back to the room's entrance.

4. Choose cheerful and uplifting colors to raise morale. A small space with dark wood paneling can be depressing. You may want to use more plants with uplights to give a feeling of depth. Avoid glare – too much light can cause irritability.

5. Make sure that open shelves are not directly pointed at you when working at your desk. The shelves have a strong piercing energy, which disrupts concentration.

6. Do not place a desk at the end of a long hallway, because there is too much energy coming down that hall which will cause illness to a person in the direct line of traffic.

Chapter Ten

Exterior Remedies for Residential & Commercial Properties to Have Good Health & Hold onto Your Wealth

Remove posts or trees directly in front of door entrances if possible. I read of a court case resulting from a city's landscaping project. Rows of trees were planted in a commercial area, and when a tree was added directly in front of a store entrance, the owner had a sudden decrease in business. Posts and trees blocking entrances hinder the flow of energy coming to you.

The electromagnetic fields of power poles interfere with and are different from the earth's natural magnetic field, which is essential in sustaining life. Placing clay pots or stones under or near these power poles is a remedy. Power poles emit a constant Fire element, and in our **Reductive Cycle Chart** in **Chapter 5**, *Figure 19*, you can see that Earth helps decrease the Fire element and in this case its negative effect! Studies have documented that children playing outside at schools located near numerous power lines or electrical towers have a higher potential to develop health challenges.

Location, location, location is an important adage. A home or apartment located very close to a fire station, police station, or cemetery, for instance, is to be avoided. Common sense tells us the noise from fire and/or police stations is disturbing, and the cemetery holds grief-type energy that affects residences nearby. Homes below streets collect more negative energy and dirt flowing from the street above. According to statistics, it's more likely to have mental illness and/or suicides occur in apartments located below the street, including residences located in the basement of a building near a street. Reasons include the lack of light, plus constant headlights directed at windows located just above the curb level. People affected by mental problems are often those living in homes with a street in the front and in the rear. Being positioned between opposing traffic is very unsettling and does not give the mind an opportunity to relax. Homes on the side of a hill, which are supported by stilts, lack a good foundation and can bring a collapse of finances or relationships to its occupants. This factor also includes apartments located over carports that provide little support for its occupants. Bedrooms over garages or carports create unhealthy conditions due to the increase in gas fumes.

Homes or buildings directly at the end of a cul-de-sac or a "T" junction, where one street flows directly into a home, can cause illness and misfortune. Many developers are now turning the ends of cul-de-sacs into parks and unobstructed areas in order to allow the energy to move freely. Homes located on the inside of a curve of the street hold in the wealth, and are protected because vehicle headlights traveling near are directed away from the home according to the shape of the street. Homes or buildings on the indent of a curve have the potential to receive negative energy, and are considered less positive since the headlights of vehicles traveling on the street point toward those buildings.

Landscaping around a home is best when it's rounded and curved lines are used. Pointed leaves create a feeling of dynamics and greater energy. Since points directed at people create a feeling of uneasiness, giving an impression of swords, avoid plants with pointed leaves near the front door where guests are welcomed or in areas where greater relaxation is desired.   Trees directly in front of doorways block positive energy from entering.

A woman who had health issues and whose husband's career was failing needed my help.   After walking the grounds, I found the cause of their troubles was a $1500 palm tree planted directly in front of the front door. The couple chose not to remove the tree. A costly mistake as misfortunes continued and within two years they divorced.

Homes with slopes flowing downward away from the structure in the front or backyard will benefit by planting a low hedge or bush, even rose bushes around the top perimeter of the property to hold in the energy and avoid money loss. The same is true of homes with long driveways. Money loss occurs as the good energy flows down the driveway and away from the home.   Often gates, posts, or landscape can be added at the top of the driveway to slow down the loss of energy that causes a decrease in wealth.

Chapter Eleven

Powerful Success Stories from Energies to Remedies – to Reinforce Your Belief in the Impact of Feng Shui

A woman contacted me because her husband and two daughters were experiencing delays after moving into their new home. I was impressed by the beautiful décor of her home and yet there seemed to be something causing the family to feel stuck. Sure enough she was correct. After taking a compass reading and working up her report, I found the permanent energy of delays in the center quadrant of her home, represented by the number 5 and accompanied by the number 9. Delays represented by the 5 are always stronger when they are accompanied by the number 9. My client's cooktop with the Fire element backed up to the center wall of the house. As I explained in the Productive Cycle, Fire melts Metal. Therefore, as she put her Metal remedy in place and then used the cooktop, the Fire would burn and decrease the energy produced by the Metal remedy.

She added a great deal of metal above her kitchen cabinets to make up for the fire of the cooktop. Her husband joked that she had so much metal she might break the cabinets. She also had a grandfather clock in the center area of the home, on the other side of the wall from the cooktop. A grandfather clock is a wonderful remedy because it has metal "workings," is always moving and makes noise. The noise helps to move energy by its vibration.

One day her friend came in the front door and commented, "What did you do to your home? It feels so good, the energy must have changed."

My client answered, "The only thing I've done is place more metal in the center of the home! You won't believe it but my grandfather clock has gained an hour, on its own. And I know nobody has touched the clock!"

The previous story is just one of many I plan to share with you in this chapter. To understand this chapter better, the following is a brief introduction to my next book: **Do It Yourself Feng Shui Guide.** This chapter gives you a preview of what types of energies might have been captured in your building when the roof was applied. In my Feng Shui Guide, I teach you how to take a compass reading on your own building and determine what types of energies exist there that are influencing your life, career, relationships, health, and prosperity. Following the compass reading, I offer you the proper remedies to move forward with what you desire in your life: how to enhance the positive energies and reduce those that do not serve you.

To understand why metal was used in our first example and why it is used most often, refer back to the **Productive Cycle Chart** from nature in **Figure 58**. I have added more advanced information to the **Productive Chart** in this example. Note each element has mathematical numbers and colors, which are used in my guide to determine the best remedies.

To remedy the energies within a building, we must determine what energies are in the space, which is done with a compass reading. For instance, there are three types of Earth energies seen in illustrated in the Productive Cycle Chart in **Figure 58** in this chapter. The 2 Earth relates to separation and/or sickness, the 5 Earth relates to delays, pain and/or struggles, and the 8 Earth relates to expansion in one or all of the following areas: health, wealth, or the addition of people in your life. The people factor could be expansion of clients, or family members, like additions to the family with a new baby or through a marriage, and/or business partnerships. With this knowledge, you can see why the number 8 is thought of as a very prosperous number in Feng Shui.

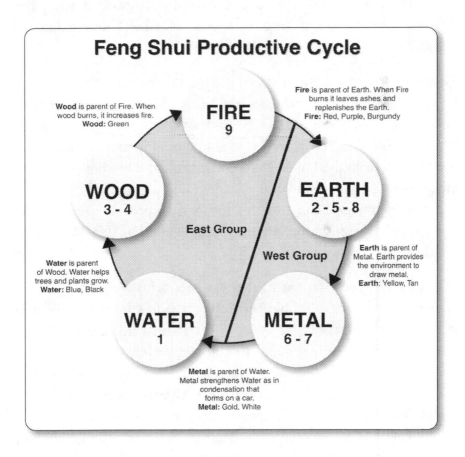

Figure 58

It is best to understand that there are no good or bad energies. The 2 energy often appears when people are moving from their home or business, which is good because it helps the business or homeowner to move on. That move could be a positive one: the business has expanded and requires a larger space, the family has downsized, has grown, or the homeowner has received a career advancement, which requires a move. I see the 2 energy appear at the front door or in the master bedroom when people are ready to sell a home, divorce, or change jobs, or the energy is at the front door or office when the business owner is making a move, whether downsizing or expanding.

To create a more harmonious environment, since we do not know how the separation or sickness may occur, or how the delays may happen, it is recommended to reduce those energies. To reduce the 2 and 5, use the **Reductive Cycle Chart**, *Figure 19*, adding a metal element in the interior. As I mentioned in my first story, my client used metal weights in her kitchen and a grandfather clock in the nearby hall, which is one of the best remedies, because it is moving metal with the pendulum swinging and has the vibration of energy when it chimes.

Metal comes from the earth, therefore reducing the 2 or 5 Earth energy, as illustrated by the **Reductive Cycle Chart** in **Chapter 5**, *Figure 19*, brings good results. The **Dominant Cycle Chart,** *Figure 20*, is also important to study in order to determine the best remedy. Due to the kitchen having the element of fire from the cooktop, according to the **Dominant Cycle Chart,** fire melts metal and therefore in order for the remedy to be effective, additional metal would be increased until seeing positive results. In this case, my client noticed her grandfather clock moving forward on its own.

By placing metal in the areas of the 2 or 5 energies in a building, you can help to reduce those types of Earth energies. When an 8 energy shows up, it is good to enhance its energy, since 8 is the Earth energy that brings in good health, wealth, and/or friends, business clients, or additions to a family. We usually strive to increase the 8 by adding Fire. Going back to nature as our source, refer to the **Productive Cycle Chart**, *Figure 58*, which demonstrates how fire replenishes or increases the earth! To learn Feng Shui and apply the advanced information, it will help to memorize the **Productive, Reductive, and Dominant Cycles** to prepare for the advanced material covered in my ***Do It Yourself Feng Shui Guide***.

One of the most desired types of buildings is the Wang Shang, Wang Shui, which means "good for health, good for wealth." Approximately 10% of houses and/or businesses are both "good for health and wealth." This fact is determined by a comprehensive Lopan Compass reading, based on mathematical numbers.

In my work with a beauty salon, the owner had her workstation in an area of the store that increased delays for her. A workstation in another area of the shop had the energy of 1 and 4. See the **Productive Cycle Chart**, which shows the 1 represented by the Water element, and the 4 represented by the Wood element. Together, these numbers represent love, creativity, and being respected in the community. When fire is added, they are also good for money. The 1 represents wealth, and the 4 creativity, love, travel, and respect. In the Chinese culture the 4 is said to represent death and often it is avoided. I have been told the number 4, when spoken in the Chinese language, sounds like the word "death." I feel it is associated with death because when a loss occurs, love and respect is usually present, plus the spirit travels out of the body when it makes its transition after death. As discussed in an earlier chapter, the number 4 is known as "The Traveler." In the very traditional practice of Feng Shui, which I practice, the 1 and the 4 are very creative and centered in love. When water is added, a new romance often manifests, especially if the 1-4 energy is at the front door. The front door indicates the potential coming to us from the outside world. This energy also brings the potential to have great respect, to be regarded as a pillar in the community.

I suggested the owner move her workstation to this area. She did and immediately afterward discovered that a previously uncomfortable situation with one of her co-workers remedied itself in a very loving way, and harmony was restored to her salon. Her co-workers and her clients seemed to have more respect for her, she told me! She continues to see an increase in her creativity, as she designs new cutting-edge hairstyles and harmony in her salon with co-workers.

Residential Properties:

That same 1 and 4 energy combination seen in the commercial beauty salon, representing love and being attractive to people, was the energy that showed up in a client's bathroom. As I've mentioned, when water is added to this 1-4 combination, it is likely that a new romance is possible for the occupants in that space. The woman called me to help her with a relationship with a married man. She said she had met him at a homeowners' meeting and he would always flirt with her. In order to stop the relationship, the water needed to be blocked. Since this was her shower we could not stop the water. When rocks are added to this energy, the romantic attraction is blocked: like placing sandbags to redirect water. This example of how rocks block water is from the **Dominant Cycle Chart Chapter 5,** *Figure 20.*

We used decorative rocks in her bathroom, and she even carried one in her pocket to the homeowners' meeting. The next day she called to tell me it worked. "He came to the meeting and sat at the table way across the room from me. Halfway through the meeting he got up and left! I can hardly believe it worked so quickly." I know she was clear on her desire and she demonstrated her intention by taking action to get the results she wanted.

I met with the owner of an entertainment agency to help her make changes to overcome the things that could be causing delays in her life after moving her business to a new location. When she phoned me, she spoke of activities that took forever to complete, and she confessed she was still waiting for her business bank checks to arrive.

I completed the Feng Shui report and she executed the remedies. A week later she phoned to tell me the delays were still occurring. After a more extensive inquiry, I discovered her employees had felt more positive in the space almost immediately after the remedies were put in place, yet she was still being personally challenged. I reevaluated my report and called her back to tell her I felt the consultation on her business was correct.

I had an idea and probed further. "Is your bedroom or your front door of your home located in the North?" I asked, and when she answered affirmatively, I asked what color she had used to decorate the bedroom. "Predominately blue," she said, and I realized her challenges were coming from delays in her master bedroom at home. When she asked for a report on her home, I found the visiting annual energy of delays was in the north where she slept. Even if she had Metal in that room to reduce the 5 Earth, representing the delays, the blue color, which represents water, would have negated her Metal remedy because, according to the **Reductive Cycle, Figure 19**, Water corrodes and reduces Metal. Once she put the correct colors and elements in her bedroom, everything began to move forward for her success in her business.

Another client with two teenage sons noticed their normally harmonious home had some negatives: their sons were always late getting out the door for school and there was an increase in unexpected expenses. The breakfast table was in the same area as the back door of the kitchen, and my client spent the most time at that table paying bills and managing the family budget. I was surprised to see that my client was not benefiting as much as she could from the very positive energy of living in a Wang Shang, Wang Shui (good for health, good for wealth) home.

The mathematical numbers in the center of her house were quite positive and had an influence on the potential for all the occupants in the home. The number combination in the center of her home was a 4 together with an 8. The 4 is good for love, respect, creativity, creative writing, and academics. Her sons may have been tardy, but they were doing well with their studies.

The placement of the 8 indicated an expansion of wealth, which required the element of Fire. In the center of the home in this area of creativity and wealth was a large fish tank, which represented the element of Water. The water was supporting the creativity of the 4 but there was no support to expand the 8 Earth representing wealth. By replacing the Water (Aquarium) with Fire, it created a balance between the 4 Wood and 8 Earth, bringing harmony to the area. When selecting a remedy, refer to the **Productive Cycle**, in this case the Fire is the element missing between the 4-Wood and 8-Earth, making that the perfect remedy to create balance in this situation. I made more suggestions about colors, and bed directions that would be more supportive, and moved some items around her home to change the elements in various areas. Where the family entered and exited the house was a 2, indicating separation and a 5 for delays. She followed my suggestions and sent me this note:

> "Good morning, Pat! Thank you for the clarification, especially in my son's room. There is so much to learn and I want to make sure I do it right. I added the metal where needed in the house and changed my curtains in the family/dining room so that the red drapes are just in the dining area and the gold valances are in the family area where we needed more metal. I moved my other son's bed, but I still need to move my bed. Well, this is what happened the day I finished making the above changes...My vacuum repair man called and said, 'No charge for the repair,' I walked out to get the mail and there was an unexpected check for $100, and a reimbursement check for fund-raiser decorations was hand delivered to me! Wild! Today I move the aquarium! Can't wait to see what happens next!"

I did a consultation on a home for another client couple before they purchased it. The center of the home, which is the most important part, indicates the potential for the entire house energy. This particular home indicated that the potential for lawsuits and legal matters would be strong, but it did not show up for a year and a half, at which time the permanent energy coming in the front door, along with the visiting energy, came together to create a potential for betrayal. The wife discovered her business partner had committed fraud involving their shared business bank account. She immediately broke off relations with the partner and ended up in court to settle the matter. My client had all the suggested remedies in place and was successful in the settlement.

Ironically, I had charted this client and her business partner when I consulted on the home, and discovered the partner was not compatible as a business partner. My client's personal Trigram was Wood and the partner's personal Trigram was Metal. Since Metal dominates Wood according to the **Dominant Cycle Chart** of nature, this event proved the relationship had not been supportive to my client from the beginning. I believe the other reason my client won her lawsuit was that she was in an East Group home, which supported her Personality East Group Type of Wood.

This client and her husband were challenged that year with the energy of arguing and legal issues. Despite being happily married for over 40 years, they were arguing more and even considering separation. With their new knowledge of Feng Shui, this couple decided to find another home, which was more supportive of their desire to have a happy family life and marriage. I asked the husband what he wanted to experience in his next home and he immediately told me, "To have good health." This home had helped him to get clear, and sure enough, when I analyzed their next home before their purchase, the numbers reflected the potential for good health along with the energy that brings a potential for lots of visitors. His wife told me that in their first year in the new home on a golf course, they experienced more visitors than in any other home, and her husband was enjoying good health and an active life.

When working with individuals, I have found that people tend to gravitate toward their personal directions, and colors that match their Trigrams, or they tend to bring their actual elements into the environment. For example, those with their personal element of Fire tend to want to put fireplaces in more than one room in the house. Wood types love wood floors and wood furniture. Those who are of the Earth Trigram often want to bring in tile throughout the house. Tile causes a problem when there is already too much Earth energy in the home, and the house Feng Shui energies have numerous 2 or 5 numbers representing Earth energy throughout.

The use of Earth—granite countertops or tile floor—in the architectural background materials of a home has a negative impact when it is in the same quadrant as the 2 and/or 5 Feng Shui energies. Earth increases the 2 and 5 energies, requiring additional Metal to reduce the added Earth used in the architectural building materials. Wood floors seem to be very compatible with any remedy as the wood is considered dormant, and needs to be a living growing plant to count as an actual Wood remedy. I have suggested bringing in area rugs to cover the tile.

Other times I have seen a husband arriving after I have rearranged the living room. He loves the placement of his favorite chair and discovers the chair has been positioned in his best facing direction according to his personal Trigram. Children intuitively select rooms and place their beds according to their best Trigram directions and the energies that are prominent in their life experiences.

Another client with "permanent house energy" of 5 (delays) at her home front door entrance also had the 5 delays for the "yearly visiting energy" at her front door. She told me that whenever she hired people they were either late or they didn't show up at all. She said on one occasion she had hired a cleaning crew who was scheduled to come, and they never showed up and did not even phone.

Before learning about her delays, I was scheduled to arrive at 5:00 PM for her appointment. I actually got there at 4:30 PM. When I started to work on her home, I realized I had forgotten my compass and had to drive back to my office to get it. When I returned it was 5:30 PM, making me a half hour late for the appointment. I had never forgotten my compass before or since. When she spoke to her husband on the phone, he laughed, "How could she forget her compass? That's like forgetting her shoes, for her."

The energy in our homes impacts all areas of our life and shows how we co-create with each other. Even though my intention was to be early for her appointment, the energy of her home was a contributing factor and impacted how our experience together played out. As more and more people become aware, together we can move forward in our spiritual growth. After all the remedies were put in place, she had workmen come and build a new garage for the home and the work went smoothly with no delays!

Another client, who is so aware of the energy, tells me she has seen how the monthly energy has affected her daily work with the stock market. At first, when I was just posting the monthly energy on my web site, I would post the energy a week or so after it came in. She started e-mailing me to remind me to post it sooner because she noticed that the energy of separation/sickness represented by the 2 came into her bedroom the month she got sick, and that same energy came to her office the month she lost the most in the stock market. Now she gets a jump on the monthly energy to place remedies in the appropriate area before it arrives each month!

Being aware can help you create more peace and harmony in your life.

Results from realtors selling homes:

A realtor who had been working to sell a home in San Diego for over three months wrote me, "Pat, I just wanted to tell you that we sold the home in San Diego in two days after we did the adjustments. We sold it to one of the two people who had the offer in on it. But their original offer was at $540,000 and they ended up paying $590,000 for the property. Anyway, I'm thrilled (even though my partner is still skeptical)!"

Another realtor wrote:

> "A spectacular new custom home that had been for sale over a year, had fallen out of escrow twice, and was just about to cause the builder's great financial loss got another chance through the efforts of my friend, Pat Sendejas. I was the new real estate agent the builders interviewed to take over the sale of this albatross.
>
> When I first viewed the property I felt there was something 'wrong.' I told the builders I would take the listing, provided I was permitted to have Pat do an evaluation. Pat did her compass readings and walked the property. Within a few minutes she 'hit the nail on the head.' She said an attorney would like the house, and later found out an attorney was one of the first buyers that fell out of escrow. She felt the energy was flowing over the edge of the property and

that a hedge would 'hold in' the energy. Towards the end of her visit she started changing a few decorator items and colors in the house.

We had only made a few of the changes she suggested. A fellow agent from out of the area drove down the driveway. He handed me his card and asked to see the house. I noticed his card had two jumping dolphins on it. Strangely, this house had a fountain in the front courtyard with two jumping dolphins. I looked at his card and knew this was going to be the sale. Well, we closed escrow on the $1,200,000 house immediately! I am a hero to the sellers especially because of Pat's knowledge, training, wisdom and caring."

A broker wrote:

"By moving a few things around in our office, a desk here, a plant there, adding some color here...some of the magic she does perform...we actually turned our business around. We merged two very good real estate companies together and we actually quadrupled our production the very month after she did the consult and we implemented the suggestions."

From another realtor:

"I listed a home that was on the market for one month and received no offers. Other homes in the surrounding area were selling quickly. This home sold

at full price just a day and a half after the consultation
with Pat."

The staircase that ended right at the front door hindered the sale of
the home above. Energy was coming down the stairs and flowing
out from the home, causing challenges for this client and showing
up in loss of prospective buyers on the home. I could not place
anything in the interior because, in order to work, it would have to
be fairly large to block the loss of energy coming down the stairs.
There was not enough room at the base of the staircase for any
additional furniture or decorative items to slow down the escaping
energy. I suggested the realtor place potted plants outside the front
door to slow down the escaping energy and hold onto good energy
for the homeowner. After taking a compass reading, I found very
good energy inside the front door, so the remedy was to bring in fire
to enhance the already good energy in that entrance. We introduced
the fire by bringing in a burgundy area rug in the front hall and she
added the potted plants outdoors. She was pleased when it sold in
less than two days at full price.

A property supervisor and investor wrote:

> "After consulting with Pat for my home, I spent over a
> month implementing her suggestions, moving
> furniture, adding various elements, and colors. Upon
> completing...putting the last item in place, to my
> surprise the house suddenly seemed to come alive."

I often find that when the elements are put in place, some people tell
me they feel a new and good type of energy around them. One
young woman reported back to me that the night she added the
Metal to her room, she felt a vibration throughout her body, as if she

were connecting with the magnetic field around her, which created a feeling of well-being.

Another client wrote:

> "Your message comes at a good time. I am currently 'letting go' of much of my old stuff – clothes, dust catchers and whatnots. It is getting easier by the day and the more I get rid of, the better I feel."

I find that letting go of things that no longer serve you helps to achieve new goals quicker. Oftentimes, when people are having difficulty making a decision to move forward into a new career or to make a decision about going forward in their lives, lots of stuff will collect. Clothes will be piled up, laundry will not get done in a timely manner, papers on a desktop will pile up, checkbooks don't get balanced, and garages fill with items that are no longer used.

People in transition, high school seniors getting ready to graduate and young college age adults sometimes have rooms that are piled with clothes or other items. Because they are not able to reach a decision that allows them to realize a direction, they can't move forward. As mail or other items pile up, they become overwhelmed and the decision becomes more difficult. With so many career choices for young adults, and with older adults being laid off, transitions can happen at any time and this expected or unexpected change can cause stress. The best solution is to work through the office or the garage or a bedroom, tackling items to be discarded or organized. Often times this is much easier to do when assisted by someone who does not have the same sentimental or emotional attachment. Don't resist asking for help and allowing assistance.

I met a woman who has a company that organizes space. She gave me some great tips on organizing my office. With an assistant I tackled my office. I reorganized all my files and purchased a shredder to get rid of papers I no longer needed. My intention was to have enough space to allow me to have a clean desktop. When the desktop is clear, you can focus on the task at hand without being distracted. To my surprise, within a week of clearing my office, I received several boxes of tapes, books, and training materials to support my business. I was delighted when I had the opportunity to pass those items on to other business associates who were glad to get them.

Getting rid of clutter is what is meant by "less is more," an historical quote from well-known architecture, Mies Van de Rohe. Children study best in an environment that has fewer distractions. Anytime you introduce something into the space that is other than the task at hand, it can cause the mind to wander onto other projects and can be quite disruptive to concentration. The myth is that we are able to multi-task and by doing so accomplish more. The truth is, to do a good job we can only focus on one thing at a time. Studies have shown that when people attempt to multi-task they do both jobs poorly. Children can best be helped by using a 3-sided study carrel around them on a desk when doing focus work, whether or not they have been diagnosed with ADD/ADHD. This device prevents disruption in the room from being a distraction when doing homework, reading, learning or taking tests.

I have come to the conclusion that trust is the biggest issue when working with my clients. Those who really want to change their lives are ready to surrender to a new way of doing things. They are willing to accept that our past belief systems have not always been based in truth. Letting go can be a challenge. By letting go, their actions demonstrate their true belief of total trust. I have come to believe that there is truly a higher power at work in all of our lives. I call upon this higher power in everything I do. My success in working with clients is because I allow this Universal energy to guide me. If you would like more information on how to begin by working with this energy, read my book...***Letting Go to create a magical life***.

All living things are made of a magnetic field with plus and minus charges. This electric field allows us to work with the Universal energy source to attract what we desire. When we feel good, coming from joy or love, this energy flows freely. When we feel sad or fearful, the Universal energy is blocked or may attract what we do not desire. When I talk with a client about getting rid of things in their environment that do not serve them, their biggest fear is that they will not have the money to purchase them again, or will never find another relationship to replace one that is not supporting them now. They forget the basic rule of, "Ask and you shall receive."

We have been given minds to find solutions and we dream about the way we would like things to be. From dreams come ideas and thoughts, and from thoughts come energy, and from energy comes our reality. As people realize how powerful human intentions and emotions are in creating our reality, we will be able to reduce war, crime, illnesses, poverty, and attract peace, harmony, and abundance.

What we focus on expands. It is important you take what information makes sense for you from Feng Shui and discard what does not feel right for you. Answers come in many forms and Feng Shui is only one way to get the answer that is right for you. If you interpret information as negative and then dwell on it, you may create more of what you do not want. Many people watch the news and become fearful that the same might happen to them and in doing so, create what they did not want. What you focus on, surround yourself with, and enjoy continues to create more of the same in your life. Our winning football teams are a great example of this focus. When teams win and continue to believe in themselves, they often continue to have a record-breaking winning streak from the momentum of that one win, which creates a new belief system. "You become like the info you listen to, the books you read, and the people you associate with," is a true and inspiring comment.

Using the Universal energy to create peace and harmony for ourselves and the world is a choice that man can make. Feng Shui has demonstrated that to me. As people get clear on what they want, and take responsibility and action to improve their life, this universal energy comes forth to support them! Whether it brings in a Feng Shui consultant to help them create a more relaxing peaceful environment, or a surgeon who removes a tumor in their body, or a massage therapist who helps them relax and reduce stress, or a nutritionist who helps them choose foods that support health, matters not. The Universe answers our requests and moves forward to support us!

In conclusion, I would like to share a message I received from a special client. She said to me at the end of her consultation, "I can improve my life because now I am more aware.   I now have the information to overcome the challenges and make choices which support me." She handed me this inspiring quote that beautifully conveyed to me how important being aware and clear are in fulfilling our dreams:

Until one is committed, there is hesitancy,

the chance to draw back, always ineffectiveness.

Concerning all acts of initiative and creation,

there is one elementary truth,

the ignorance of which kills countless ideas and splendid plans:

That the moment one definitely commits oneself,

then Providence moves too.

All sorts of things occur to help one

That would never otherwise have occurred.

A whole stream of events issues from the decision,

Raising in one's favor all manner of unforeseen incidents and meetings

And material assistance,

Which no man could have dreamed would come his way.

Whatever you can do or dream, begin it!

Boldness had genius, power, and magic in it.

Johann Wolfgang von Goethe

About the Author

Pat Sendejas has always been passionate about personal environments. When she was seven and spending the night at a friend's home, her idea of fun was telling her friend: "Let's go rearrange your parents' living room!"

Pat continued to listen to her calling and graduated from UCLA's Environmental Interior Design and Architecture Program. She started her own interior design business in 1977, and when asked to teach at a local college, she completed a B.A. degree in Art from Cal State University Northridge. She was an award winning Kitchen Designer, a participant in the Conejo Valley Interior Design Showcase House, and worked on Model Homes for Camino Real Country Estates in Agoura Hills, California.

When a friend gave Pat a book on Feng Shui in 1996, she immediately knew it was something she wanted to learn to combine it with her interior design practice. She felt a strong foundation in Feng Shui, especially in the Traditional Compass School, which is thousands of years old and based on science, observation of nature and mathematics, was extremely important. With her extensive knowledge of the subject, she has taught Feng Shui at colleges, consults with clients, and still gives seminars around the country.

She has been the selected speaker for a wide range of events, from conventions to corporate meetings, including such diverse groups as LAX Homeland Security Department and Independent Community Bankers of America. Her client list also includes Farmers' Insurance Group Corporate, Hyatt Hotel, and Celebrity and Costa Cruise

Lines. Author of several books and an experienced radio talk show host, Pat has been featured in numerous magazines and newspapers, among them: Woman's World Magazine, Estylo Magazine, In Magazine, the Los Angeles Daily News, and Ventura County Star News.

Pat feels that Interior Design is complete when Feng Shui and the qualities of the individual using the space are considered together.

A resident of Southern California, Pat is married to a retired L.A. City firefighter. She has two adult sons, and her favorite pastime is being with her grandchildren. Being in nature is a passion and taking her grandkids to the Santa Barbara Zoo with husband, Sal, gives her the greatest pleasure.

When Pat was learning to write her name in elementary school, she discovered that if she wrote her name backwards and held it up to a mirror, she could read it. Her concerned father called for a meeting with Pat's teacher, who reassured him, "No worries, she just looks at the world differently than most."

Direct all correspondence to author:

PAT SENDEJAS

Post Office Box 4514 Westlake Village, CA. 91359-1514

E-mail: Pat@Speaker4Change.com.

Website: www.Speaker4Change.com

For information about your environment visit:
Website: www.WithinYourSpace.com